W9-BKO-297

Great Americana

A Winter in the West.

VOLUME I

Charles Fenno Hoffman

A Winter in the West.
By a New-Yorker

VOLUME I

by Charles Fenno Hoffman

READEX MICROPRINT

31743

COPYRIGHT © READEX MICROPRINT CORPORATION, 1966

ALL RIGHTS RESERVED

LIBRARY OF CONGRESS CATALOG CARD NO. 66-26345

MANUFACTURED IN THE UNITED STATES OF AMERICA

917.304
H699w
v.1

Foreword

Most early descriptions of western America were composed by individuals who were not writers by profession. An exception was *A Winter In The West*, written by Charles Fenno Hoffman, a man who attained distinction in American letters as an editor, poet, and novelist during the first half of the nineteenth century. Partly for reasons of health, Hoffman resigned the editorship of the *Knickerbocker* in 1833 and set out alone on horseback for a winter tour of the Midwest. As he had lost a leg in a childhood accident, the venture was an audacious one. From various points along the route he sent back letters containing his impressions of the country for publication in the New York *American*. The letters aroused a considerable interest. After more than thirty had been printed, it was decided to hold the rest and to publish them, together with the earlier ones, in book form. The book appeared in 1835. Hoffman won praise both in America and in England for his ability to capture what was most typical of each locality he visited.

Everywhere he went Hoffman looked upon the country first with a poet's eye. It came as a disappointment to him that so few persons who lived in the midst of such natural beauty appreciated their good fortune. "Alas," he concluded," the majority of mankind have no innate sense of beauty and majesty." But the loveliness of the countryside was by no means his exclusive preoccupation. He gloried in the history of the region, short though it was, sought our battlefields and places of historic interest, and listened raptly to stories associated with the events of an earlier day. The bustling commercial activity of towns like Pittsburgh, Detroit, St. Louis, and Cincinnati filled him with admiration. When a system of canals was completed linking the Great Lakes with the Mississippi River, he foresaw a still more rapid development of the region. Eastern capital was urgently needed to finance the canal construction, however—a fact which Hoffman tried to publicize. The West also needed more women. "The number of males in proportion to females on the frontier is at least five to one," he estimated. The relationship of whites to Indians was another problem which required solution. The Americans were less successful than the French had been, perhaps owing to their differences of approach. With the French the "government did nothing, individuals every thing; with us, government attempts every thing, and individuals frustrate all."

When he reached St. Louis, Hoffman had hoped to proceed up the Missouri River with a party of the American Fur Company. He had to renounce the project because some of those in the party objected to having "a chiel amang them takin notes." Hoffman therefore headed back East and was home again some eight months after his departure.

The *Dictionary of American Biography* provides a short sketch of Hoffman's life. For more detail, particularly regarding his tour of the Midwest, see Homer F. Barnes, *Charles Fenno Hoffman* (New York, 1930), pp. 47-57, 63-67.

A

WINTER IN THE WEST.

BY A NEW-YORKER.

Where can I journey to your secret springs,
Eternal Nature ? Onward still I press,
Follow thy windings still, yet sigh for more.
GOETHE.

IN TWO VOLUMES.

VOL. I.

NEW-YORK:

PUBLISHED BY HARPER & BROTHERS,
NO. 82 CLIFF-STREET.

1835.

[Entered, according to Act of Congress, in the year 1835, by CHARLES
F. HOFFMAN, in the Office of the Clerk of the Southern District
of New-York.]

PREFACE.

SEVERAL of these letters have already appeared in the New-York American;—the favourable reception they have met with has induced the writer to complete the series and publish them in the present form. In preparing them for publication, he has thought proper to illustrate some of the facts contained in them, by observations derived from other sources or made subsequent to their date. These additions the author has preferred to place in an appendix, rather than imbody them with the original matter, as he feared that whatever attraction his sketches of scenery and manners might possess would evaporate upon throwing them into a different form, and their chief merit as first and faithful impressions would be lost. The eloquent writings of Mr. Flint, the graphic sketches of Judge Hall, and the valuable scientific researches of Mr. Schoolcraft, Professor Keating, and the lamented Say, have already made the regions described in these pages well known to the public; but there is an ever-salient freshness in the theme of " The Far West," which prevents its becoming trite or tiresome; and as the author believes himself to be the first tourist who has taken a winter view of scenes upon the Indian frontier, he trusts that this circumstance will impart some degree of novelty to his descriptions in that quarter, while the romantic beauty of the region described nearer home will bear its own recommendation with it.

A

WINTER IN THE WEST.

LETTER I.

Easton, Pennsylvania, Oct. 17.

My dear ——,

My journey has not as yet furnished an incident
worthy of being entered into the diary of the most
unambitious tourist. Still I take the first opportunity of fulfilling the promise given, when starting
on the wide excursion I meditate, of writing to my
friends from the different stages of the route, and
describing its features with sufficient minuteness
for those who take an interest in my letters to accompany their writer in his wanderings. With
which of my friends, with whom breathing, my
dearest ——, can I better commence my little narrative than with one who will only regard its details
with the eye of affection—unmindful alike of their
want of intrinsic interest, and the unattractive form
in which they may be conveyed, so they be but
a faithful record of my wayfaring.

Our route hither from New-Brunswick (or *Rougemont*, as some one proposes calling it from the colour of the soil) was as uninviting as a rainy, disagreeable day, bad roads, and a country neither fertile nor picturesque could make it. Occasionally, indeed, glimpses of the Raritan gave animation to the scene, as, sparkling restlessly between its cold brown banks, it rushes like an ill-matched bride from their dreary embrace to sully its pure waters in the marsh through which it passes to the sea. These glimpses, however, are but transient, and for the remainder of the drive but few natural objects presented themselves to induce one to dispute that quaint Indian tradition which avers, that when the Manitou had finished making the rest of this mighty continent, he slapped from his fingers the mud and gravel which form this part of New-Jersey.

We reached a straggling village, called Jacksonville, about nightfall, at a low-roofed unpretending looking stone inn, where we had a capital supper —of which buckwheat-cakes, not quite so large as a New-York grass-plat, formed no mean ingredient —and slept in sheets of snow. To this auspicious characteristic their properties in other respects bore a resemblance, as I afterward discovered, which might readily be dispensed with. I awoke at dawn, with rheumatic pains in every part of my bones, and found, what had escaped me the night before, that every particle of the covering of my bed was as wet as if it had been transferred at once from the hands of the laundress to my bed, without undergoing the dilatory process of drying. I was glad to get at once into the saddle, and mounting one of the led horses, it took a warm trot of a dozen miles to relax my aching muscles, and make me anticipate my breakfast with any thing like satisfaction.

The morning, though cloudy, broke beautifully. The country, as we approached the borders of Pennsylvania, increased in interest. Richly wooded hills, with here and there a fertile slope evincing a high state of cultivation, shone out beneath the fitful sky. The streams from the uplands were more frequent, and their currents flowed with heightened animation. The farm-houses, too, became more substantial in appearance ; and their gray-stone fronts, standing sometimes in a clump of sycamores aloof from the road, betokened the quiet comfort of their inhabitants. The roads indeed were worse than indifferent—but that, though a sudden rain soon set in, did not prevent our enjoying the clouded but still beautiful landscape.

We crossed the bridge over the Delaware to

Easton at about two o'clock, and driving to the famous inn of Mr. White, the Cruttenden of these parts, were soon safely housed in his hospitable establishment. Having breakfasted at eleven, we ordered dinner at five, and strolled out to see the lions of the place. The roar of a waterfall was the first thing which attracted my notice, and following the sound I soon found myself near the great dam over the Lehigh, where, at its junction with the Delaware, back water is created for the sake of supplying the Lehigh Canal. The pond thus formed, which, with its abrupt banks, and frowning limestone cliffs wooded to the top, might almost pass for a small natural lake, is filled with small craft,—the lubberly-looking ark, and sharp clean-built Durham boat, lying moored by the shore, with numerous light skiffs drawn up near them. I easily procured one of the latter, and shooting under the chainbridge which spans the Lehigh, the wind and current carried me in a moment past stone wharves heaped with anthracite coal to the brink of the dam. The sudden slope of the water here had an awkward look about it which reminded me vividly of a peep I once took from a row-boat into " the Pot" at Hell-gate, when its screwing eddies carried the eye with a strange fascination deep into the boiling caldron. Bending heartily to my oars, I was glad to leave the glassy brim that sloped so smoothly to destruction.

The operations of a keel-boat working up against the rapid current of the Delaware next caught my attention. She had four men to manage her—the roughest, hardiest looking set of fellows I ever saw, broad-shouldered and brawny, with complexions like copper, and having no covering to their heads but coarse curly hair, matted so thick that it looked as if the stroke of a sabre might almost be turned by it. The strength and agility of these fellows is very striking, as they stride along the gunwale with their long poles, and twist themselves into all sorts of positions while urging their unwilling craft against the foaming current. After they had gained and passed the lock, and floated into the basin where my boat was lying, I could not help rowing near theirs to examine their iron frames more narrowly. I was just making up my mind that such a collection of bold, reckless, impudent faces as were borne by these worthies, I had never before seen, when my surmises in physiognomy were fully confirmed by a volley of billingsgate which one of them let fly at me. It being perfectly in character I was of course much amused at it, and by gently lying on my oars and looking at him, incensed my amiable acquaintance to a degree that was irresistibly ludicrous. I waited till he was exhausted; and when he wound up by "damning my spectacles," I reflected with Dr. Franklin, that it was not the first time they had saved my eyes; and mentally consigning the fellow to the tender mercies of Hall and Trollope, pulled for the berth of my little shallop, and soon after regained my quarters.

I think you would be much pleased with Easton. The situation of the village itself is eminently happy—almost picturesque—and the country around it delightful. Imagine a lap of land, not quite a mile square, embosomed among green hills, bounded by two fine rivers and a pretty mill-stream —the straight rectangular streets now terminating with a bold bluff, descending so immediately to their very pavements that its rocky sides, skirted with copsewood, seem to overhang the place, and again either washed by one of the streams that determine the site of the town, or facing some narrow ravine which leads the eye off through a wild vista to the open country; and the remarkably flourishing and well-built appearance of the village itself, with its two bridges, and the extensive works of the Morris and the Lehigh Canals adjacent,—and you have almost as favourable a combination of rural objects and city improvements as could well be effected on one spot.

The chief buildings are the County Court-house, situated in a fine square in the centre of the place, and the Lafayette College, which, from a commanding position over the Bushkill, faces one of the principal streets. The latter is a *Manual labour* institution (a term I need hardly explain to you), recently incorporated, and likely to flourish under the energetic superintendence of the Rev. Mr. Junkin, its able principal. Easton, as you are probably aware, is celebrated for the rich mineralogical specimens found in its vicinity. The salubrity of the place, as I am informed by an eminent physician, is remarkable; and one can readily believe in its exemption from most of the fevers of the country, from the fact of there being no woodcock ground within five miles of the Court-house. The site was chosen and the town-plat laid out by Penn, a town-monger who, if he did cut his plans with a scissors from paper, as a recent foreign traveller has hinted was the case with regard to Philadelphia, had certainly a happy knack in adapting the model to the locality. The descendants of the great colonizer are still said to own property in Easton, while the peaceful members of his brotherhood, in our day, bless his

memory when turning up the jasper arrow-head
within the precincts of the village; and thank
Heaven for the teacher whose gentle counsels
withdrew for ever from this lovely valley the red
archers that shot them.

Eagerly as I am now treading on the steps of
that fated race to their fleeting home in the far
west, with what emotions of pleasure shall I not
count every returning mile that will bring me near
you.

LETTER II.

Rodrocksville, Pa., Oct. 19.

The last red hues of sunset were just dying over the western extremity of the road we had long been following, when a herd of cattle, under the guidance of a woolly-headed urchin, collecting indolently around an extensive farm-yard, reminded us alike that it was time to seek shelter, and that one was at hand. A few paces farther brought us to the door of a large stone building, displaying, with the usual insignia of an inn, an unwonted neatness in all its out-door arrangements: unharnessing our four-footed fellow-travellers, we proceeded, in spite of the threatening outcry of a huge bandog chained at its entrance, to bestow them comfortably in a stable near at hand. A Canadian pony, with a couple of goats, the companionable occupants, seemed hardly to notice the intrusion; and leaving an active mulatto ostler to reconcile any difficulties which might arise between our pampered steeds and a sorry-looking jade which just then entered to claim a share of the comforts at hand, we soon ensconced ourselves before a crackling wood-fire in the comfortable apartment where I am now writing.

Every mile of our route to-day has given some new occasion to admire the scale upon which farming is conducted in Pennsylvania. The fences, indeed, are not remarkable for the order in which they are kept; but while the enclosures themselves are tilled with a nicety which preserves the utmost verge of a field from shooting up into weeds or brushwood, the barns into which their harvests are gathered are so spaciously and solidly built, that they want only architectural design to rival in appearance the most ambitious private mansions. Stone is almost the only material used here in building; and the massive profusion in which not only the barns, but the smallest outhouses upon the premises of these sturdy husbandmen, are piled upon their fertile acres, is such as would astonish and delight the agriculturist accustomed only to the few and frail structures with which the farmers of most other sections of our country content themselves. The establishment of our host is admirably supplied with these lordly appurtenances in which a true tiller of the soil may so justly show his pride. The huge cathedral-looking edifice which towers above his farm-yard would make as proud a temple

as could be well reared to Ceres, even by Tripto-
lemus himself.

The most picturesque country we have yet seen
is that immediately around Easton. Indeed, the
first view that opened upon us when gaining the
brow of a wooded hill, about half a mile from the
town, was so fine as to make us forget the regret
with which we had a few moments before bid
adieu to our prince of landlords and his blooming
daughters.

The Lehigh, for about half a mile in extent,
lay in the form of a crescent beneath us—a wooded
ravine striking down to either horn, and undulating
fields, some ruddy with buckwheat stubble, and
some green from the newly-sprouting wheat, filled
up the curves. A gray stone-barn stood here and
there on an eminence against the bright morning
sky, while sheltered below on the alluvial flats
formed by the river, a white-walled cottage might
be seen reposing by its cheerful current. The
Lehigh Canal, winding through the valley, side by
side with the river, like a younger sister bent on
the same errand, added not a little, when viewed
at such a distance, to the beauties of the scene.

We took our breakfast at Bethlehem, and availing myself of an hour's delay while the horses
were feeding, I left my friend puzzling himself over

a German newspaper, and strolled off to look at the village. It is a place of considerable interest, not less on account of its ancient and peculiar appearance than the Moravian institutions which have rendered it so celebrated. I was fortunate enough to meet with Mr. Seidel, the principal of the female seminary, who, upon my asking him some trivial question about that excellent establishment, offered, in the most polite manner, though I was wholly unknown to him, to show me through the building. It is a plain stone structure, of some eighty feet in length, subdivided internally into lecture-rooms and dormitories like some of our colleges; one range of small apartments being used entirely as *washing* rooms by the pupils, and having all the necessary furniture for that purpose neatly arranged about each. These, like every other part of the establishment, have their peculiar superintendent, and standing thus distinctly by themselves, form an essential feature in the economy of the institution, and with the extensive play-grounds in the rear of the building, evince the attention which is paid to the health and personal habits, as well as the intellectual improvement of its inmates. I was shown into the school-rooms of the several classes, and had ample opportunity, as the ruddy bright-eyed occupants rose to receive my conductor, to observe the happy effect of the life they led upon their personal appearance. A fresher, fairer assemblage of youthful beauty has rarely greeted my eyes. Several of the apartments were furnished with pianos, and my curious entrance into these smiling domains startled more than one young musician from her morning's practising. I was, as you may suppose, a little, a very little, confused at being thus exposed to the full broadside gaze of a hundred "boarding-school misses." This, though, however it might forbid my examining their features in detail, did not prevent me from observing that their general expression was happy and natural —two sources of attraction not so very common in the sex, but that they will still strike one even when displayed, as was the case in this instance, in mere children.

I subsequently visited the burial-ground of the place, which I contemplated with no slight interest. The disposal of the dead is as true a test of civilization in a community as the social relations of the living. The taste which embellishes life passes with the arts attendant upon it, from one nation to another, like a merchantable commodity; but the sentiment that would veil the dreariness of the grave, and throw a charm even around the sepulchre, that would hide the forbidding features of

that formal mound, and shelter the ashes beneath
it from contumely—this is a characteristic springing from some peculiar tone of national feeling, and
radically distinctive of the community that pos-
sesses it. The philosopher, it is true, may sneer at
our care of this bodily machine when the principle
that gave it motion has ceased to actuate it; but
how stolid is he who can look upon the ruin of a
noble edifice, even though made irretrievably desolate, with apathy; or who would not fence up
from intrusive dilapidation halls hallowed, whether
by the recollection of our own personal enjoyments
or the memory of the great and good of other times.
It is one and the same feeling which arrests our
steps beneath a mouldering fortress, and which
induces a pilgrimage to the tomb of a departed
poet; which kindles our indignation against the
plunderer of the Parthenon, that "titled pilferer
of what Time and Turks had spared;" and which
makes it ready to consume the wretches who tore
the bones of Milton from his sepulchre.

The calm sequestered privacy of the Bethlehem
burial-ground would have satisfied even the particularity of Sir Lucius O'Trigger, whose encouraging suggestion to his non-combative friend Acres,
"that there was good lying in the Abbey," shows that
he had an eye to his comfort in these matters. It

stands aloof from the bustling part of the village, near a noble church, which still faces on one of the principal streets. The approach from the church, which has grounds of its own, in the form of an ornamented terrace around it, is through a narrow green lane. At the entrance of this, shaded by a clump of willows, stands a small stone building called, I believe, from the purposes to which it is applied, " The Dead House." Here the bodies of the dead are deposited for many hours previous to interment. The head is left uncovered, and life, if by any possibility it be yet remaining, has a chance of renewing its energies before the jaws of the tomb close for ever over its victim. I looked through the grated windows, but saw nothing except an empty bier in the centre, and several shells adapted to coffins of different sizes leaning against the wall. With the usual perversity of human nature, I half regretted that the solemn chamber was at the moment untenanted, and passed on to the place of which it is the threshold.

There my eye was met by the same neat appearances and severe taste which seem to prevail throughout the economy of the Moravians. The graves, arranged in rows, with an avenue through the centre dividing the males from the females, are in the form of an oblong square, flattened on the top, with a small slab reposing in the centre.   On this are cut simply the name of the deceased, and the dates of his birth and death—a meager memorial—but enough : and I could not help—after deciphering a number of these moss-covered stones, upon which the dews of more than a century had wept—turning with distaste from a few flaring marble slabs at the farther end of the yard, upon which the virtues of those beneath were emblazoned in the most approved modern forms.

I left the spot, thinking it a pity that a greater number of trees did not, by shading the grounds, complete their beauty, and felt willing that the young locusts which skirt them round should have time to fling their branches farther towards the centre, before I should have occasion to claim the hospitality of the place.

Need I say how truly, until then, I am

Yours.

LETTER III.

Harrisburgh, Pa., Oct. 22.

I write to you from the banks of the Susquehannah. A dull steady rain prevails out of doors, and after wading through the mud about the purlieus of this place for an hour, I am glad to be housed at last for the rest of the day. I see the capital of Pennsylvania under every disadvantage, but still am pleased with it. Although a city in miniature (and this contains only four or five thousand inhabitants) is generally odious to one who has resided in a metropolis—reminding him perhaps of Goose Gibbie in jack-boots, at the Review of Tillietudlem—there is much in the appearance of Harrisburgh to reconcile the most captious to its assumption of civic honours. The manner in which the place is laid out and built, the substantial improvements going forward, and the degree of wealth and enterprise manifested in those already made, and above all, its beautiful site, make it an exception to the generally uninteresting character of country towns.

The chief part of the town lies on a piece of champaign land, about 40 feet above the level of the Susquehannah; the handsomest street in the place, though occupied chiefly by petty tradesmen and mechanics, verging on the waters of that lovely stream.   The other streets run at right-angles to, and parallel with, the river, which is nearly straight, except where it washes the town with a graceful bend near the suburbs of either end.   Facing the Susquehannah at the upper part of the town, and only a few hundred yards from the river, is a sudden elevation rising into a level platform, about 60 feet above the surrounding plain.   Upon this eminence, fronting the river through a broad street, stands the capitol and state buildings, containing the chief public offices.   The centre edifice, and one standing detached on either side, are all ornamented with Grecian porticoes, and their size, their simple design, and just architectural proportions, would make an imposing display, and impress a stranger favourably until he ascertained the paltry material of which they are built.   But I defy any one, unless he may have written sonnets to Time in the ruins of Babel, to have one respectful association with a structure of *brick*.   Putting the perishable nature of the material entirely out of the question, although a sufficient objection to its use in a public building, its size alone is fatal to effect in a structure of any pretension. For it is massiveness in the details as well as in combination, which delights the beholder in architectural forms : and the pyramids of Egypt themselves, if reared of boyish marbles, though they might be so ingeniously put together as to awaken curiosity, could never inspire awe. The disciple of Malthus perhaps might busy himself in calculating how many urchins it took—supposing every one in the dominions of Cheops to have contributed his mite to complete the fabric—but where would have been all those ingenious surmises with which antiquarians, since the days of old Herodotus, and who knows how many centuries before, have puzzled the brains of their readers ? Where would be that reverence with which mankind in every known age have regarded these monuments of the power of their race in the early vigour of its creation ? Where would be the awe with which we now regard these artificial mountains that rear their stupendous forms in proportions that mock at modern art ; and, rivalling in their heaped-up rocky masses the masonry of Nature herself, speak of the labours of a race for whom the Mastodon of our own continent would have been a fitting beast of burden ?

What a singular perversion of taste is that existing in the towns and villages through which I am passing, which induces the inhabitants to make their barns and cow-sheds of solid stone, and their ornamental buildings of brick and stucco. I sometimes see Gothic churches of the first, and Grecian fronts of the last; and these not unfrequently planted in the midst of a cluster of gray mansions, whose towering gables, huge stone-buttresses, and deep-cut narrow windows make the former show like some pert poplar thrusting his dandy figure among a clump of hoary oaks. Still one cannot but admire the air of comfort--I might almost say of opulence—which prevails throughout the country I am traversing. This, in the village of Reading, through which we passed yesterday, is particularly the case. It has a population of about 7,000 inhabitants; and the numerous coaches filled with passengers which pass daily through it, the wagons loaded with produce that throng the streets of the place, and the rich display of goods and fancy articles in the shops, give Reading a most flourishing appearance. It is prettily situated on the Schuylkill, with a range of high rocky hills in the rear; but its position wants the picturesque beauty of Harrisburgh. Here the Susquehannah is, I should think, full half a mile wide. It is studded with wooded islets, and flows between banks which, though not very bold in themselves, yet rise with sufficient dignity from the margin, and blend with the undulating country, until the arable slopes and sunny orchards are bounded by a distant range of mountains.

The prospect from the capitol is, I am told, uncommonly fine ; but the thick mist which limited my view to a very narrow compass while walking along the banks of the river an hour ago, has hitherto prevented me from trying the view. I shall visit the spot from which it is to be had in the morning.

Yesterday I had, for the first time, the gratification of hearing a sermon pronounced in German— the common language of this part of the country. I walked some distance through a pelting shower to the church in Womelsdorf; and though the preacher was prevented by sudden indisposition from giving more than the exordium of his discourse, I was sufficiently delighted with his clear, mellow enunciation, and the noble sound and volume of the language which he spoke in all its purity, to regret most deeply an often-deferred resolution of mastering that manly tongue. One must think more strongly in such a muscular language. I have frequently had occasion to admire the expressiveness of the German in poetry, when Goëthe or

Schiller were quoted by others, but I had not till now a conception of the effect in oratory of that language which gave energy to the torrent of Luther's denunciations, and richness to the flow of Melancthon's eloquence. I listened, it is true, not understandingly, but like one who admires the compass of an instrument, though ignorant of the air that is produced from it. I conceived, however, that I could follow the preacher in his preliminary address; and, indeed, the tone of fervid feeling and unaffected solemnity in which it was made would have impressed, if it did not bear along, the most ignorant listener. The congregation, owing to the weather, was but small. The two sexes sat apart from each other, and had a separate entrance to the building. We were not aware of this at our entrance; and as a matter of good taste, my friend and I took our seat among the ladies, when an active master of ceremonies, probably the sexton, insisted upon showing us to another place, and with difficulty induced us to change our situation, after we had once or twice declined with thanks what we conceived to be an officious act of politeness on his part. The young *Vrounties* appeared to regard our interchange of civilities with particular interest; and I am half persuaded that had we not struck our flag to the gentleman-usher just when we did, the womankind (as Jonathan Oldbuck presumes to call the suzeraines of the lords of creation) would have risen to a man (Hibernicé) in our favour, and insisted upon keeping us among them.

I shall keep open this letter till to-morrow evening, and add every thing I have to say on this side of the Alleghanies—for the present, good-night.

October 23.—The rain still continued when I left Harrisburgh this morning, and the view I promised myself from the capitol was not to be had. My disappointment at not having seen more of the Susquehannah is not slight, and the feeling is enhanced by a delicious glance I caught of its waters in the sunlight, as the clouds parted for a moment, just as a turning of the road shut out the view behind us. I almost grew melancholy while recalling with a sort of home feeling the delight with which, years ago, I first beheld its sources, to remember now that it was the last stream running eastward, that I should see for a long time to come. And then those calm, gentle waters, which flow as smoothly as the verse of him who has immortalized them, once seen are never to be forgotten nor passed again without interest. The Susquehannah has its birth in one of the loveliest of lakes, and bears with it the impress of its parentage where-ever it wanders—the bright green surface and transparent depths below, the winding current which, unbroken by cascade or rapids, whether it steals through the rich fields and beautiful glens of Otsego, or smiles on the storied vale of Wyoming, loiters alike beside its fertile banks, as if reluctant to pass them on its long journey to the ocean. For grandeur of scenery, indeed, the Hudson far surpasses it; and where is the stream that can match that lordly river! But there is a gentle beauty about the Susquehannah which touches without striking, and wins while you are unawed. The one, like a fair face lit up with glorious intellect, commands and exacts your homage; with the other, as with features softened with tenderness, you leave your heart as an offering.

We are now, you will observe, on the main road from Philadelphia to Pittsburgh, and as our stopping-places, instead of being in those mongrel establishments, half inn, half farm-house, will probably be at the stage-coach offices along the route, but little opportunity will offer for observing the manners of the residents. Thus far I have no reason to complain of the want of civility of the people among whom I have passed the last week; with the exception of the amusing little incident detailed in my first letter, not a circumstance has occurred to qualify this remark. The general appearance of the country east of the mountains, you have already gathered from the two previous letters. Latterly we have travelled so continually in the rain that I have had no opportunity of seeing it to advantage. But the only change I observe in the face of the country is that, instead of being broken up into small hills, where forest and cultivation are most happily mingled—as around Bethlehem—the vales here spread out into plains, and the high grounds receding, swell off till they show like mountains in the distance. I miss, too, those fine barns upon which I have dwelt with so much pleasure; nor do the better fencing and spruce-looking dwelling-houses compensate for the loss of the imposing appearance of such huge granaries in an agricultural country. I thought, when first observing the change, and marking the herds of cattle and droves of sheep that sometimes throng the roads, that we had got at last completely into a grazing region. But the delicious wheat-bread met with at the humblest inns, with the little stock to be seen in the fields seems to indicate that such is not the case. It seems odd in a country so thickly settled, where one meets a hamlet at every two or three miles, with scattering houses at frequent intervals between them, that wild animals should be yet abundant. But I was told at Bethlehem that it was not uncommon to kill bears upon the neighbouring hills; and a gentleman informed me this morning that they frequently drove deer into the Susquehannah, within a few miles of Harrisburgh. I can account for it only by the fine forests which are everywhere left standing isolated in the midst of cultivated tracts, making so many links in the chain of woodland from mountain to mountain across the country, and tempting the wild animals, while it extends their range, to venture near to the settlements.

You may be aware that, in New-York, owing to the wholesale manner in which clearings are made, the deer are swept off with the forests that sheltered them, and retreating into the mountain fastnesses of the northern counties, or the rude wilds of the southern tier, are there crowded so thickly as to be butchered for their skins. In the former region, while fishing, within a few weeks since, among the picturesque lakes which stud the surface of the country, I have seen the deer grazing like tamed cattle on the banks. It was a beautiful sight to behold a noble buck calmly raising his head as the skiff from which we trolled approached the margin; and then, after standing a moment at gaze, toss his antlers high in air, and with a snort of defiance bound into the forest.

Farewell. You shall hear from me again so soon as we pass the Alleghanies, the first purple ridge of which I can already see limning the sky in the distance. In the mean time, I will note down any thing of interest which catches my eye, and endeavour to give you hereafter some idea of the lofty land-mark which, before you read this, will be placed between us.

LETTER IV.

Bedford, Pa., Oct. 24th, 1833.

We have commenced ascending the Alleghanies. A cold, difficult ride among the hills has brought us at last to an excellent inn in the little town from which I write. A blazing fire of seasoned oak in a large open stove, sputters and crackles before me ; and, after having warmed my fingers, and spent some twenty minutes in examining an extensive collection of Indian arms and equipments, arranged around the room with a degree of taste that would not have disgraced the study of Sir Walter Scott, I sit down quietly to give you my first impressions of this mountain region.

We entered these highlands yesterday ; S., who values himself upon being a great whip, driving his ponies up the ascent, and I, as usual, on horseback. It was about an hour before sunset that we commenced ascending a mountain ridge, whose deep blue outline, visible for many a long mile before we reached the base, might be mistaken in the distance for the loftier rampart of which it is only the outpost. The elevation, which showed afar off like a straight line along the horizon, became broken in appearance as the eye, at a nearer view, measured its ragged eminences; but it was not till we were winding up a broad hollow, scooped out of the hillside, and through which the beams of the declining sun played upon the fields and farm-houses beyond, that the true character of the adjacent region opened upon us. The ridge we were ascending still rose like a huge wall before us, but the peaks, which had seemed to lean against the clear October sky, like loftier summits of the same elevation, now stood apart from the frowning barrier, towering up each from its own base—the bastions of the vast rampart we were scaling. Each step of our ascent seemed to bring out some new beauty, as, at the successive turns of the road, the view eastward was widened or contracted by the wooded glen up which it led. But all of these charming glimpses, though any of them would have made a fine cabinet picture, were forgotten in the varied prospect that opened upon us at the summit of the ridge. Behind, towards the east, evening seemed almost to have closed in upon the hamlet from which we had commenced our ascent, at the base of the mountain; but beyond its deepening shadow, the warm sunset smiled over a thousand orchards and cultivated

fields, dotted with farm-houses, and relieved by
patches of woodland, whose gorgeous autumnal
tints made them show like the flower-beds of one
broad garden.   Southwardly, the sweeping upland
which here heaved at once from the arable grounds
beneath us, while it swelled higher, rose less suddenly from the plain.   At one point the brown
fields seemed to be climbing its slopes, while here
and there a smooth meadow ran like the frith of a
sea within its yawning glens ; and now again peak
after peak of this part of the range could be traced
for leagues away, till the last blue summit melted
into the sky, and was finally lost in the mellow
distance.   Such, while our horses' heads were
turned to the north-west, was the rich and varied
view behind us—the prospect from the Catskills is
the only one I can recollect that rivals it in magnifi-
cence.   But another scene, more striking, though
not so imposing, was also at hand,—a ridge like
that we had just crossed rose before us ; but beneath our very feet, and apparently so near that it
seemed as if one might drop a stone into its bosom,
lay one of the loveliest little valleys that the sun
ever shone into.   It was not a mile in width, beautifully cultivated, and with one small village reposing in its very centre ; the southern extremity

seemed to wind among the lofty hills I have already attempted to describe, but its confines towards the north were at once determined by a cluster of highlands, whose unequal summits waved boldly forth in the purple light of evening. The sun, which had now withdrawn his beams from the scene behind us, still lingered near this lovely spot, and his last glances, before they reached the hill-side we were descending, flashed upon the windows of the village church, and, creeping unwillingly up its spire, touched with glory the gilded vane; then from the sweeping cone of a pine above us, smiling wistfully back on the landscape he was leaving, yielded it at last to coming night.

The descent of the mountain, from its multiplied windings, consumed more time than I had anticipated. The faint rays of a young moon were just beginning to compete successfully with the fading tints of day, before we had neared the village sufficiently to hear the lowing of cattle, and the shrill shout of the cow-boy, driving his charge homeward; and her maturer beams were softened by the thin haze which rose imperceptibly from a brook winding through the valley, before we reached our destination for the night. The occasional jingling of a wagoner's bells in the distance, and the merriment of a group of children playing by the moonlight in a grassy field near the stream, were the only sounds that broke the stillness of the scene as we drove up to the door. I thought of the happy valley of Rasselas, and wondered whether the inhabitants of this secluded spot could really ever wish to wander beyond its beautiful precincts.

The gradual, successive, and delicious blending of lights, as I have attempted to describe them, under which I first beheld the little valley of M'Connelsville, will, doubtless, account for much of my admiration of it; and indeed some of its features were changed, and not for the better, when viewed under a different aspect the next morning. A sharp north-easter, in spite of the barriers which had seemed to shelter it, drove down the valley; a cold drizzling rain, with its attendant mist, shut from view the mountain tops around; and the village dwellings, lining one long narrow street, and now no longer gilded with the hues of sunset, nor standing clearly out in the silver light of the moon, showed like the miserable hovels they were; the snug stone-house where I had passed the night seemed to be almost the only tolerable building in the village, and I was not sorry to pass its last straggling enclosure, and commence ascending the arduous height beyond.

The summit of this attained, another valley, about double the width of that just passed, lay before us; and as the rain subsided at noon, leaving a gloomy lowering day, we could discover through the cold gray atmosphere ridge succeeding to ridge, leaning like successive layers against the western sky.

A half day's rough ride among these wild ravines brought us at last to the banks of the Juniata, along which an excellent road is cut for some distance. The stream, though in the midst of scenery of the boldest description, keeps its way so calmly between its rocky banks, that the dead leaf upon its bosom floats many a mile before a ripple curls over its crisped sides, and sinks the little shallop to the bottom. We dined near nightfall at a small hamlet, known, from a brook that runs through it, as " The Bloody Run." The stream which bears this startling name is a rill so small that its existence is barely perceptible, as it creeps through the pebbles across the road, and hastens to hide its slender current in the long grass of an orchard beyond; but its waters will be pointed out by the villager with interest, so long as they dampen the channel where they once flowed in all the pride and fulness of a mountain torrent.

It was several years before the Revolution, according to the statement given to me by one of those distinguished persons who in country towns always figure after a great storm or freshet, as the "oldest inhabitant of the place," that a large party of colonists, on their march towards Fort Du Quesne, were here cut off by the Indians. The ambushed foe had allowed the main body to pass the brook and surmount the heights beyond; and the rear-guard, with the cattle they had in leading for the use of the troops, were drinking from the stream, when the onslaught was made. The Indians rushed from their covert, and burst upon their victims so suddenly that fifty whites were massacred almost before resistance was attempted. Those who were standing were dropped like deer at gaze by the forest marksmen; and those who were stooping over the stream, before they even heard the charging yell of their assailants, received the blow from the tomahawk which mingled their life's blood with the current from which they were drinking.

The retribution of the whites is said to have been furious and terrible. The body of men in advance returned upon their tracks, encamped upon the spot, and after duly fortifying themselves, divided into parties, and scoured the forest for leagues. My informant, who gave me only the traditionary account of the village, could not tell how long this wild chase lasted; but that it must have been fear-fully successful is proved, not only by the oral record of the place, but by the loose bones and Indian weapons which are at this day continually found amid piles of stone in the adjacent woods; the Indians probably returning to the valley after the storm had passed over, and heaping their customary *cairn* over the bodies of their dead kindred.

What a contrast was the peaceful scene I now beheld to that which the place witnessed some seventy years ago! A train of huge Pennsylvania wagons were standing variously drawn up, upon the very spot where the conflict was deadliest; the smoking teams of some were just being unharnessed, a few jaded beasts stood lazily drinking from the shallow stream that gurgled around their fetlocks, while others, more animated at the near prospect of food and rest, jingled the bells appended to the collars in unison with their iron traces, which clanked over the stones as they stalked off to the stable. To these signs of quiet and security were added those true village appearances which struck me so pleasingly on my approach to M'Connels-ville. A buxom country-girl or two could be seen moving through the enclosures, bearing the milk-pail to meet the cows which were coming in lowing along the highway, while the shouts and laughter of a troop of boys just let loose from school came merrily on the ear as they frolicked on a little green hard by. My companion stood in the midst of them, holding a piece of silver in his fingers, while a dozen little chaps around him were trying who could win the bright guerdon by standing on one leg the longest. The ridiculous postures of the little crew, with the not less ludicrous gravity of my friend, who was thus diverting himself, of course, put an end to my sober musings; but I could not help, while advancing to the scene of the sport, fancying for a moment the effect of the war-whoop breaking suddenly, as ere now it often has, upon a scene apparently so safe, sheltered, and happy.—Good-night.

P.S.—*Somerset, Oct.* 26*th.*—You have read in the newspapers of the recent destruction of this place by fire; it must have been large and flourishing, judging by the extensive ruins which I have just been trying to trace by the frosty light of the moon now shining over them. The appearances of desolation here are really melancholy; the inn where we put up is the only one left standing, out of five or six, and it is so crowded with the houseless inhabitants that I find it difficult to get a place to write in.

We are now in the bosom of the Alleghanies: the scenery passed to-day is beautiful, most beautiful. The mountains are loftier, as well as more imposing in form, than those which skirt these wild regions eastwardly; whichever way the eye directs itself, they are piled upon each other in masses, which blend at last with the clouds above them. At one point they lie in confused heaps together; at another they lap each other with outlines as distinct as if the crest of each were of chiselled stone : some, while the breeze quivers through their dense forests, rear their round backs, like the hump of a camel, boldly near; and some, swelling more gradually from the vales below, show in the blue distance like waves caught on the curl by some mighty hand, and arrested ere they broke on the misty region beyond. Then for their foliage ! the glorious hues of autumn are here displayed in all their fulness, and brilliancy, and power—volume upon volume, like the rolling masses of sunset clouds, the leafy summits fold against the sky— calm at one moment as the bow of peace, whose tints they borrow; and at another flaming like the banners of a thousand battles in the breeze.

But why should I attempt to describe what baffles all description? The humblest grove of our country is, at this season, arrayed in colours such as the Italian masters never dreamed of; and woods like these assume a pomp which awes the pencil into weakness. Such forests, such foliage were unknown when our language was invented. Let those who named the noble-sounding rivers that reflect their glories supply words to describe them.

Farewell. I shall write to you next from Wheeling, Virginia; and if you do not think me tedious, will touch again upon the beauties of the region through which I am now passing.

LETTER V.

Wheeling, Virginia, October 29th.

I used to think our sea-board climate as capricious as it could well be; but the changing skies under which we have travelled for the last three days convince me that nowhere is the office of weather-cock less of a sinecure than in the region through which I have just travelled. Yet I do not complain of the weather—far from it; I consider myself peculiarly fortunate in having, during a three days' ride over the Alleghanies, seen that fine mountain-district under every vicissitude of climate; and though the cold has at times been severe—the harsh rains any thing but agreeable for the time—the Indian summer heat almost sultry, and, lastly, the *snow* most unseasonable, I could not, if I had made my own private arrangements with the clerk of the weather, have fixed it upon the whole more to my satisfaction. The still cold frosty mornings gave a vigour and boldness of outline to the mountain-scenery, that extended its limits and heightened its effect. The rains which an hour afterward washed the changing leaves brightened their tints for the noonday sun which

followed; and the warm mist of evening imbued
the landscape with a Claude-like mellowness that
suited the rich repose of evening among the hills.

As for the snow, nothing could be more beautiful
than the effect of it at this season in the woods.
We had two flurries on successive days, each of
which, after covering the ground about an inch in
depth, was succeeded by a bright glowing sky.
The appearance the woods then presented it
would be almost impossible to describe to you.
Call up in your mind the brilliant and animated
effect produced by a January sun shining through
a leafless grove, over the fresh white carpet that
has been wound among the trees during the preceding night. How do the dead branches smile
in the frosty sunbeams; how joyously does every
thing sparkle in the refracted light! Now imagine
the tinted leaves of autumn blushing over those
rigid limbs, and reflecting warmth upon the dazzling
mantle beneath them—green, gold, and purple,
scarlet, saffron, and vermilion; the dolphin hues
of our dying woods glistening in the silver shower,
and relieved against a surface of virgin whiteness.
Let the scene lie, if you choose, among mountains
clothed with forests as far as the eye can reach—
their billowy forms now sweeping off in vast curves
along the sky, and now broken by ravines, through

which a dozen conflicting lights climb their shaggy sides; or, not less striking, let it be a majestic river, whose fertile islands, rich alluvial bottoms, and wooded bluffs beyond are thus dressed at once in Autumn's pomp and Winter's robe of pride, and you can hardly conceive a more beautiful combination. Such was the aspect under which I crossed the last summit of the Alleghanies yesterday, and such under which I viewed the Ohio this morning.

The fine undulating country between the mountains and this place, especially after passing the post-town of Washington, on the borders of Pennsylvania, left me nothing to regret in the way of scenery after crossing the last ridge this side of Somerset. And yet nothing can be more exhilarating than a canter over those heights on a bracing October day. The sudden breaks and turns of the mountain road open new views upon you at every moment, and the clear, pure atmosphere one breathes, with the motion of a spirited horse, would " create a soul beneath the ribs of death," and rejuvenate Methuselah himself. One must once have been a dyspeptic to estimate to the full that feeling of exulting health. For my own part, however philosophers may preach up the sublimity of intellectual pleasures, or poets dilate upon the delights of etherealizing sentiment, I confess that I hold one

good burst of pure animal spirits far above them
all. On horseback, especially, when life quickens
in every vein, when there is life in the breeze that
plays upon your cheek, and life in each bound of
the noble creature beneath you; who that has felt
his pulses gladden, and youth, glorious indomitable
youth, swelling high above manhood's colder tide
in his bosom—who would give the rush of spirits,
the breathing poetry of that moment, for all the
lays that lyrist ever sung—for all the joys philoso-
phy e'er proved?   This, I know, must appear a
shocking doctrine to "the march of mind" people;
but as they are presumed to go on foot, they are
no authority on the subject.   Apropos of pedes-
trians, though your true western man generally
journeys on horseback, yet one meets numbers of
the former on this side of the Alleghanies.   They
generally have a tow-cloth knapsack, or light
leathern valise, hung across their backs, and are
often very decently dressed in a blue coat, gray
trousers, and round hat.   They travel about forty
miles a day.

The horsemen almost invariably wear a drab
great-coat, fur cap, and green cloth leggins; and
in addition to a pair of well-filled saddle-bags,
very often have strapped to their crupper a convenience the last you would expect to find in

the wardrobe of a backwoodsman, videlicet, an umbrella. The females of every rank, in this mountainous country, ride in short dresses. They are generally wholly unattended, and sometimes in large parties of their own sex. The saddles and housings of their horses are very gay; and I have repeatedly seen a party of four or five buxom damsels, mounted on sorry-looking beasts, whose rough hides, unconscious of a currycomb, contrasted oddly enough with saddles of purple velvet, reposing on scarlet saddle-cloths, worked with orange-coloured borders. I have examined the manufacture of these gorgeous trappings at the saddleries in some of the towns in passing. They much resemble those which are prepared in New-York for the South American market, and are of a much cheaper make, and far less durable, than those which a plainer taste would prefer. Still the effect of these gay colours, as you catch a glimpse of them afar off, fluttering through the woods, is by no means bad. They would show well in a picture, and be readily seized by a painter in relieving the shadows of a sombre landscape.

But by far the greatest portion of travellers one meets with, not to mention the ordinary stage-coach passengers, consists of teamsters and the emigrants. The former generally drive six horses before their enormous wagons—stout, heavy-looking beasts, descended, it is said, from the famous draught horses of Normandy. They go about twenty miles a day. The leading horses are often ornamented with a number of bells suspended from a square raised frame-work over their collars, originally adopted to warn these lumbering machines of each other's approach, and prevent their being brought up all standing in the narrow parts of the road.

As for the emigrants, it would astonish you to witness how they get along. A covered one-horse wagon generally contains the whole worldly substance of a family consisting not unfrequently of a dozen members. The tolls are so high along this western turnpike, and horses are comparatively so cheap in the region whither the emigrant is bound, that he rarely provides more than one miserable Rosinante to transport his whole family to the far west. The strength of the poor animal is of course half the time unequal to the demand upon it, and you will, therefore, unless it be raining very hard, rarely see any one in the wagon, except perhaps some child overtaken by sickness, or a mother nursing a young infant. The head of the family walks by the horse, cheering and encouraging him on his way. The good woman, when not engaged as hinted above, either trudges along with her husband, or, leading some weary little traveller by the hand far behind, endeavours to keep the rest of her charge from loitering by the wayside. The old house-dog—if not chained beneath the wagon to prevent the half-starved brute from foraging too freely in a friendly country—brings up the rear. I made acquaintance with more than one of these faithful followers in passing, by throwing him a biscuit as I rode by, and my canine friend, when we met at an inn occasionally afterward, was sure to cultivate the intimacy. Sometimes these invaluable companions give out on the road, and in their broken-down condition are sold for a trifle by their masters. I saw several fine setters which I had reason to suspect came into the country in this way; and the owner of a superb brindled greyhound which I met among the mountains, told me that he had bought him from an English emigrant for a dollar. He used the animal with great success upon deer, and had already been offered fifty dollars for him.

The hardships of such a tour must form no bad preparatory school for the arduous life which the new settler has afterward to enter upon. Their horses, of course, frequently give out on the road; and in companies so numerous, sickness must fre-

quently overtake some of the members.   Nor
should I wonder at serious accidents often occur-
ring with those crank conveyances among the
precipices and ravines of the mountains.   At one
place I saw a horse, but recently dead, lying beneath a steep, along the top of which the road led ;
and a little farther in advance, I picked up a pocket-
book with some loose leaves floating near the edge
of the precipice.   It recalled the story of Car-
denio in Don Quixote, with the dead mule and the
rifled portmanteau lying a few yards apart, among
the rocks of the Sierra Morena ; and we almost
expected to see the grotesque figure which so excited the noble emulation of the worthy knight,
leaping from rock to rock in the same guise that
the admirable pencil of Cervantes has assigned to
him.   The apparition did not show itself, however ;
and we left the pocket-book at the nearest inn, to
be disposed of according to the claimants that
might appear.   These mountains, though occasionally thus cut up by precipitous glens, are still
by no means rocky—as would appear from the
fact of the inhabitants hunting deer on horseback,
through woods which would be almost impervious
to a pair of city-bred legs.   The modus operandi
is very simple.   The hunters collect in a troop—
drive the deer in a circle—and then shoot from the

saddle. You may remember something of the same kind described in Waverley. The soil must in general be indifferent, according to what was told us by the keeper of a turnpike-gate, who claimed to be the father of twenty-seven children! I asked this worthy *paterfamilias* if the country was healthy. "Healthy, sir!" he replied, "that it is—healthy and poor—ten people run away where one dies in it." The soil improves much after leaving the mountains; and we crossed some rich bottom lands when fording the Youghioghany and Monongahela Rivers,—the former a branch of the latter, and both fine pebbly streams, navigable at certain seasons of the year.

About thirty miles from Wheeling we first struck the national road. It appears to have been originally constructed of large round stones, thrown without much arrangement on the surface of the soil, after the road was first levelled. These are now being ploughed up, and a thin layer of broken stones is in many places spread over the renovated surface. I hope the roadmakers have not the conscience to call this Macadamizing. It yields like snow-drift to the heavy wheels which traverse it, and the very best parts of the road that I saw are not to be compared with a Long Island turnpike. Two-thirds indeed of the extent we traversed were worse than any artificial road I ever travelled, except perhaps the log causeways among the new settlements in northern New-York. The ruts are worn so broad and deep by heavy travel, that an army of pigmies might march into the bosom of the country under the cover they would afford; and old Ixion himself could hardly trundle his wheel over such awful furrows. Perhaps I was the more struck with the appearance of this celebrated highway from the fact of much of the road over the mountains having been in excellent condition.— There is one feature, however, in this national work which is truly fine,—I allude to the massive stone bridges which form a part of it. They occur, as the road crosses a winding creek, a dozen times within twice as many miles. They consist either of one, two, or three arches; the centre arch being sprung a foot or two higher than those on either side. Their thick walls projecting above the road, their round stone buttresses, and carved key-stones combine to give them an air of Roman solidity and strength. They are monuments of taste and power that will speak well for the country when the brick towns they bind together shall have crumbled in the dust.

These frequently recurring bridges are striking objects in the landscape, where the road winds for

many miles through a narrow valley.   They may
be seen at almost every turn spanning the deep
bosom of the defile, and reflected with all their
sombre beauty in the stream below.

The valley widens within a few miles of Wheeling, and the road strikes into the hill-side, whose
crooked base it has long been following.   It soon
begins to be cut out of the solid rock, and the
ascent is rapidly accelerated.   Above, on the right,
the trees impend from a lofty hill over your path,
and far below you see the stream, so long your
companion, gleaming through a small cultivated
bottom, which shows like a garden to the eye.   It
is girdled by steep hills, and seems, with its single
mill and one or two farm-houses, to be shut out
from all the world.   Advance but a pistol-shot,
and you look into the chimneys of Wheeling.
The OHIO is beneath your feet.   The town lies in
so narrow a strip along the river, that, from the
ridge on which you stand, you will hardly notice
its crowded buildings ;—that first view of the
lovely river of the west is worth a journey of a
thousand miles.   The clear majestic tide, the fertile
islands on its bosom, the bold and towering heights
opposite, with the green esplanade of alluvion in
front, and the forest-crowned headlands above and
below, round which the river sweeps away, to

bless and gladden the fruitful regions that drink its
limpid waters,—these, with the recollections of
deeds done upon its banks—the wild incidents and
savage encounters of border story, so immediately
contrasted with all the luxuries of civilization that
now float securely upon that peaceful current,—
these make up a moral picture whose colours are
laid in the heart, never to be effaced :—no man will
ever forget his first view of the Ohio.

I descended with regret from the elevation which
afforded this noble prospect, and plunging into the
smoky town below, am now comfortably quartered
in the best tavern in the place. I shall remain
here only till a steamboat comes along, and will
write to you next from Pittsburg.

LETTER VI.

Pittsburg, November 3d.

I passed an evening most agreeably at Wheeling, with two or three prominent members of the Bar, who were distinguished by that courtesy and cordial frankness which mark the western Virginian. A venison steak and flask of old **Tuscaloosa** (the relish and flavour of which would have been tocsin to the soul of Apicius, and made Anacreon uneasy in his grave) gave cordiality to the meeting. It was my first introduction into western society, and I could hardly have been initiated under better auspices, as I went under the wing of an Ohio gentleman, whose warm hospitality and endearing social qualities, united as they are to distinguished professional talents, seem to make him a universal favourite in this region. The conversation, animated, various, and instructive, would supply material for a dozen letters. But the nervous expressions, and almost startling boldness, of western phraseology would lose half its vividness and power when transferred to paper. I found myself, however, catching occasionally something of the characteristic tone of those around me, and my new friends gave so encouraging a reception to each fresh fledged sally, that I live in the humble hope of being able to express myself with sufficient propriety by the time I reach the really outer west, to prevent people from detecting at once the early disadvantages I have laboured under, in living so long in a land where every lip lisps homage to mincing Walker, and each tongue trembles in terrorem of terrible Johnson. In that event I may have both scenes and characters to describe, when we meet, such as would now split my pen in telling.

Wheeling is one of the most flourishing places on the Ohio. The immense quantity of bituminous coal in the adjacent region, which may be had merely for the digging, gives it great advantages as a manufacturing place, while the rich back country and favourable position on the river, especially in low water, when steamboats find Pittsburgh difficult of access, make the town a place of active trade. It lies in two parallel streets, beneath a hill extending along the river, and its smoky purlieus, when viewed from within, except to the eye of the man of business, are any thing but attractive. The principal tavern of the place, wherein I lodged, is well supplied with bedchambers, and parlours, and a comfortable reading-room, where the leading papers in the Union are taken. The attendance too, all the servants being blacks, is very good. Among them, a perfect treasure, in the shape of a genuine old Virginian negro, must not be forgotten. The features of Billy (for that is the name of my sable friend) are an exact copy of those generally introduced into Washington's picture when he is painted with his favourite groom in attendance. I piqued myself considerably upon having discovered the likeness, when I afterward found that the worthy Ethiop had actually been "raised," as he expressed it, in the Washington family. He is a professing member of the Baptist church, and I was much interested, while talking with the newly converted heathen (for such he called himself prior to the "change"), to find how the precepts with which he had lately become indoctrinated assorted with the ideas he had been brought up in as a slave ; religion seemed only to have strengthened the bonds which held him to his master. "This new light," he said, "showed the old nigger" (I give his exact words) "that to whatever station God pleased to call him, there it was good for the old nigger to be." I was told that he was rigidly attentive to his spiritual duties, and as for his worldly ones, I never met with a more thorough-bred and respectful servant. He is among the last of a race once numerous in the Old Dominion, but now fading from the face of the earth. *Sero in cœlum redeas*, and when thy dusky soul takes flight, thy name be immortal Billy, let thy statue, carved in ebony, be set up in Hudson's door-way, and a memoir of thy life flare in each intelligence-office in the Union.

It was with no slight regret that I parted with my friend S., when stepping on board a pretty steamboat, called the Gazelle, to take my passage up the river; his foreign travel, and various opportunities, have given him habits of observation which, with a dash of humour and ready flow of fine spirits, constitute a capital travelling companion. His literary tastes are well known to you; and I should not be surprised if, at a future day, he should distinguish himself as another member of his family has so happily done, by committing to the press a few notes of his wanderings.*　I left him waiting for the downward boat, and we parted, promising to meet again in a few months at New-Orleans— each of us in the mean time traversing regions from which the kingdoms and principalities of Europe might be carved out and never missed.

The snow of yesterday yet covered the ground,

---

* This expectation has not been defeated, as " Notes on Spain, by a citizen of Louisiana," are among the new publications announced in England.

as we rubbed along the shores of the Ohio; and those pictured woods, with the morning sun gleaming through their tall stems, and glistening on the powdered tree-tops, were indescribably beautiful. The islets, particularly where the hues of the foliage were most vivid, shone like shields of silver blazoned with no mortal heraldry. Before noon, however, the sun absorbed every particle of earth's fragile covering. The warm mist of Indian summer succeeded, the river became like glass, every island floated double upon its bosom, and each headland seemed to drop its cliffs against a nether sky. The harsh panting of our high-pressure engine, or the sudden flapping of a duck's wing, as he rose abruptly from under the bow of the boat, were the only sounds abroad. The day so still, so soft, and summery, seemed like the sabbath of the dying year.

The evening came on calm and mellow, and the broad disc of the moon slept as quietly on the fair bosom of the Ohio, as if her slumbers there had never been broken by the war-whoop, or reveille, from the shadowy banks around.

Having always been a faithful seeker after border legends and traditions of the old Indian wars, I could not help calling to mind a few of those with which my memory was stored, and endeavouring to lay their proper *venue* in the scenes around me. Unfortunately, however, there was no one aboard of the boat who could enlighten me in this respect; and though particularly anxious to see the spot where the doughty Adam Poe, like another Jack the Giant-killer, vanquished a Wyandot large enough to swallow him at a mouthful, I could only, by asking the distances, from time to time, along the river, guess at the point, among others similarly associated with romantic adventure.*

The peculiar scenery of the Ohio has been so graphically described by Flint and Hall, in their various writings upon the West, that I will not detain you by dwelling minutely upon its features. The prominent characteristics of the river, are a clear winding current, studded with alluvial islands, and flowing between banks, which now lie in a level esplanade of several hundred acres, elevated perhaps fifty feet above the water, and again swell boldly from the margin to the height of three or four hundred feet in headlands, which, when the mists of evening settle upon the landscape, wear the appearance of distant mountains; when I add that an occasional farm-house, with its luxuriant orchards and other enclosures, may be found along

* See note A.

the smaller " bottoms," while the larger ones are frequently enlivened by a bustling village, reposing in their ample bosoms, you have the main features of the Ohio, as I have seen it between Wheeling and Pittsburg. The windings of the river present, at every turn, some of the most beautiful views in the world; but the regular alternations of " bluff" and " bottom" give such a sameness to the landscape, that unless familiar with the points of the country around, one might be dropped in a dozen different places along the river, and not be aware of a change in his situation. Nature seems to have delighted in repeating again and again the same lovely forms, which she first moulded in this favourite region.

We passed Rapp's flourishing settlement, called Economy, during the day, but only near enough to see the regular arrangement of the square brick dwellings, standing about twenty feet apart, on broad streets which intersect each other at right angles; the factories with their high cupolas, and the thriving orchards, and young vineyards, which stretch along the banks of the river beyond the suburbs. I may hereafter, if I have time to visit it, give you some account of the present condition of this settlement, which belongs to a society organized, I believe, partially upon Mr. Owen's plan. The site of the town was formerly a favourite rallying-point for the Delaware Indians, under their chief *Monahatoocha*, whose council-fires once blazed where now the smoke of a dozen factories rolls from the chimneys of the German emigrant. What a contrast between the toilsome race, whose clanking machinery is now the only sound that greets the ear as you near the shore, and the indolent savage, or laughter-loving Frenchman, who once stalked along the borders, or danced over the bosom of the beautiful river.

> " How changed the scene since merry Jean Baptiste
>   Paddled his pirogue on La Belle Rivière,
>   And from its banks some lone Loyola priest
>   Echoed the night song of the voyageur."

The afternoon sun shone warmly on the eastern bank of the river, where the increasing number of farm-houses, and occasionally a handsome seat tastefully planted among them, with its hanging garden, not unfrequently kissed by the current of the river, indicated our approach to the city of Pittsburg,—the eastern head of the Mississippi Valley, and the key to the broad region bathed by its waters. Our course lay for a few moments among islands, that seemed to bloom in never-dying verdure, and then, as we escaped from their green cincture, the tall cliffs of the Monongahela, blackened by the numerous furnaces that smoke along their base, and pierced in various points with the deep coal shafts that feed their fires, frowned over the placid water. It was just sunset, and the triangular city, with its steeples peering through a cloud of dense smoke, and its two rivers, spanned each by a noble bridge, that seem, when thus viewed, a reflection of each other, lay before us. On the right, the calm and full tide of the Monongahela, flowing beneath rocky banks, some three hundred feet in elevation, was shaded by the impending height, and reflected the blaze of a dozen furnaces in its sable bosom. On the left, the golden tints of sunset still played over the clear pebbly wave of the Alleghany, and freshened the white outline of a long, low-built nunnery, standing on a sudden elevation back from the river. The dusty city lay in the midst, the bridges springing from its centre terminating the view up both rivers; while the mists of evening were rapidly closing in upon the undulating country that formed the background of the picture.

Truly, the waters have here chosen a lovely spot for their meeting, and it was but natural that such a stream as the Ohio should spring from such a union. Looking backward now I could see that river, like a young giant rejoicing in its birth, sweeping suddenly on its course, but turning every moment among its green islands, as if to look back till the last upon the home of its infancy.

We entered the Monongahela, and disembarked a few hundred yards from the site of the old fort Du Quesne. The river was some *twenty-five* feet lower than usual, and giving my baggage to a dray-man in attendance, I ascended the bank, and soon found my way through streets, which, though neither broad nor cheerful-looking, are still well-built, to the Exchange Hotel on the opposite side of the town. Here I am now housed, and, after delivering my letters and looking further about the place, you shall have the result of my observations.

LETTER VII.

Pittsburg, November 10th.

It was a bright, bracing autumnal morning, as I rode out of Pittsburg with a party of gentlemen, for " Braddock's Field." Our route followed the course of the river; sometimes keeping the rich bottom on its borders, sometimes ascending a hilly ridge. The height commanded a wide view of the river, now winding between steep hills, whose shadows met as they slept upon its quiet bosom, now expanding into a small lake, so completely landlocked that it seemed to have no connection with the bright stream seen flashing through the meadows farther on. After catching more than one glimpse like this of the landscape behind us, whose sunny fields contrasted beautifully with the dense smoke of Pittsburg in the back-ground, we struck into a ravine cutting the road hitherto pursued at right angles. Winding now through a deep dingle, where the path-side was festooned with vines, we crossed a small brook, and reached the shore of the Monongahela opposite to a broad alluvial flat, whose high cultivation and sunny aspect contrasted vividly with the wild and secluded dell from the mouth of which we beheld it. The road next led for some distance through a wood on the immediate bank of the river, and then gaining the more public highway, we found ourselves, after passing several comfortable farmhouses, immediately in front of the battle-ground.

It is cut up now by three or four enclosures,—the field upon which the fight was hottest lying nearly in the centre, bounded on one side by the road, and having its opposite extremity about a quarter of a mile from the river, with a wooded flat intervening. Beyond this flat is the ford over which Braddock passed. The ground about two hundred yards from the ford rises in a gradual slope for some two hundred yards more, and then swells suddenly into a tolerably steep hill, the summit of which may be half a mile from the river. On the middle slope lies the central field of action, to which I have already alluded. It is seamed with two shallow ravines, or gullies,* which run parallel with each other towards the river, and are about gunshot apart.

* These gullies, from having been long subjected to the action of the plough, are now but little more than mere swales, three or four yards in breadth, and as many feet in depth.

In these ravines, concealed by the underwood,
and protected by the trunks of trees felled for the
purpose, lay the French and Indian force. It
amounted, according to the best accounts, to only
500 men,* and was commanded by a subaltern
officer, who suggested this ambuscade as a desperate expedient to save Fort Du Quesne from the
overwhelming force that was about to invest it.
The road of Braddock lay immediately between
these enfilading parties.

It was about midday when he passed his troops
over the river in detachments of two hundred and
five hundred, followed by the column of artillery,
the baggage, and the main body of the army, commanded by himself in person. The latter had
hardly time to form upon the flat below, when a
quick fire in front told them that the two detachments which had gained the first slope were
already engaged. They advanced in double
quick step to sustain them ; but the whole seven
hundred gave way, and falling back upon the advancing troops, struck panic and dismay throughout the ranks in a moment. The confusion seemed
for a while irremediable. Some fired off their ammunition without aim or object, and others, deaf to

* See note B.

the commands and exhortations of their officers, flung away their arms, and gave themselves up to despair.

Burning with the disgrace, and eager to shame their soldiers into better conduct, the British officers advanced singly and in squads among the bullets of the enemy. They were slaughtered indeed like sheep; but their men, whose retreat had been partially cut off by the river, rallied at the galling sight. The cool determination of young Washington, who had already had two horses shot under him, and his clothes pierced with bullets, imparted some steadiness to their feelings, and they seemed ready to protract the fight to the best advantage. The madness of Braddock, however, whose weak mind took fire at the idea of receiving a lesson from a provincial youth of three-and-twenty, destroyed every remaining chance of success. He insisted upon his men forming on the spot, and advancing in regular platoon against an enemy which none of them could see. Line after line, they would hardly attain a pace between the fatal ravines before they would be mowed down like grass. But their courage was now up, and though broken, and in some disorder, they attempted with courageous pertinacity, to secure each step they gained, by protecting themselves behind the trees, and returning the murderous fire of the foe after his own fashion. The military coxcomb who commanded this ill-fated band would not hear of this. He stamped, raved, and swore, called his men cowards, and struck them with his sword. In the mean time, an evolution was being executed in another part of the field which might yet have turned the fate of the day. Capt. Waggoner, of the Virginia forces, pushed his fine corps, consisting of eighty men, beyond the voice of his besotted commander, to the summit of the hill, with the loss of only three men, in running the fearful gauntlet to attain that position. A fallen tree here protected his brave little force, and enabled him to rake the ravines, which lay at right angles to his natural breastwork, to great advantage. But the Virginians were mistaken by their English friends below for a new enemy, and fired upon so furiously that they were compelled to retreat from their position with the loss of two-thirds of the corps, killed by their misguided comrades. Thus was the strife protracted for nearly three hours, when the fall of Braddock, after losing 700 men and forty officers, put an end to the blind conflict. Fifteen hundred men, being thrice the number of the enemy, escaped to tell the havoc of the day, and spread consternation and horror throughout the province.

The military chest of the British, containing 25,000 pounds, fell into the hands of the enemy, as did likewise an extensive train of artillery, with ammunition and provisions to a large amount. Among those who perished on this disastrous occasion were Sir William Shirley, a son of the Governor of New-York, and Sir Peter Halket, with one of his sons, and other officers of distinction or promise. Sir John St. Clair and Lieut. Colonel Gage, afterward well known in our revolutionary history, were among the wounded. Many of the officers fell at the first onset; but Braddock himself had advanced some distance up the hill when he received the mortal wound, of which he died a day or two afterward. The stump of the tree against which he leaned after being struck is still pointed out in a wheat-field above the highway. He was carried off by the flying troops, and dying with many others on the march, was buried beneath the road over which his men were retreating.

The Letters of Horace Walpole, recently published, have thrown a light upon Braddock's character that should put an end at once to all the forbearance hitherto exercised in commenting upon his share in this bloody transaction. The misfortunes of the hot and misguided, but high-bred and gallant soldier were to be touched upon with lenity : the selfish rashness and utter destitution of military capacity of the broken-down gambler should be stigmatized as they deserve. Yet it is not from Walpole alone that we learn what a presumptuous blockhead England sent hither to mend his ruined fortunes, at the risk of the best blood in the country ; for, though history has dealt so leniently with his character, the records of those times paint the man in his true colours ; and so gross was his ignorance, and so offensive his pride, that he seems to have been hated and despised from the moment he assumed the command of the forces destined hither. The interest with which I viewed the battle-ground has kept me all the morning looking over a mass of documents relating to those times, and, as they are still before me, I am tempted to make more than one extract. " We have a general," writes the brave and accomplished Sir William Shirley, from the camp at Cumberland, to his friend Governor Morris, at Philadelphia—" we have a general most judiciously chosen for being disqualified for the service he is employed in, in almost every respect.

I am greatly disgusted at seeing an expedition (as it is called) so ill-concerted originally in England, so ill-appointed, and so improperly conducted since in America. I shall be very happy to have to retract hereafter what I have said, and submit to be censured as moody and apprehensive. I hope, my dear Morris, to spend a tolerable winter with you at Philadelphia." Poor Shirley ! He never saw that winter. He was shot through the brain at the very commencement of the battle.

There is a lively comment on this letter in the well-known reply of Braddock to the prudent suggestions of Washington, previous to the battle, when he urged his commanding officer to push an advanced guard into the wood before his main body :—" By G—d, sir, these are high times, when a British general is to take counsel from a Virginia buckskin !"

The speech of an Indian chief before the council of Pennsylvania, preserved among the State records at Harrisburg, offers an illustration still more striking. " Brothers," said the sagacious ally of the colonists, " it is well known to you how unhappily we have been defeated by the French on Monongahela : we must let you know that it was all of the pride and ignorance of that great general that came from England. He is now dead ; but he was a bad man when he was alive. He looked upon us as dogs, and would never hear any thing that was said to him. We often endeavoured to advise him, and to tell him of the danger he was in with his soldiers; but he never appeared pleased with us, and that was the reason that a great many of our warriors left him, and would not be under his command. Brothers, we advise you not to give up the point, though we have in a measure been chastised from above. But let us unite our strength. You are very numerous, and all the governors along your eastern shores can raise men enough. Don't let those that come over the great seas be concerned any more. They are unfit to fight in the woods. Let us go by ourselves—*we that come out of this ground.* WE may be assured to conquer the French." The military counsel and support of this intrepid and high-souled chieftain would have been heard at least, even if it did not prevail, in the camp of Napoleon. Does it not make you indignant to think how it was trampled upon and insulted by such a creature as Braddock? One would have thought that the insolent spirit of the London debauchee would have felt rebuked into nothingness before the genius of the warrior of the woods. But let the man rest; he had that one virtue to which all weak minds bow—courage.

And so had the Hessians that in a subsequent war were bought to fight against us for sixpence a day. May we rather meet, again and again, such brave mercenaries in battle, than be marshalled once to the fight by a leader whom even valour cannot shelter from deserved contempt.

The field of this celebrated action presents, of course, a very different appearance from what it did when Braddock's followers were here hunted through the forest. It is, however, but a few years since the wood was cut from the side-hill, and traces of the conflict are still occasionally discovered in the grove along the margin of the river below. I was told, too, that bones and bullets, with rusted knives, hatchets, and bayonets, were sometimes even yet turned up by the plough on the spot where the fight was hottest. The central enclosure was cleared about seventeen years since. It was heavily timbered at the time, and they tell in the neighbourhood that the teeth of the saws in the mills adjacent were continually broken upon the balls imbedded in the ancient trees. Quantities of human bones and rust-eaten weapons are said to have been found beneath the surface of the soil, when the plough first invaded this memorable wood. I picked up a bone myself, which my horse's hoof disengaged from the soil; but my skill in anatomy not being sufficient to determine whether it was even human or not, I returned the mouldering relic to the dust, of which it was rapidly becoming a part. It was an animated and interesting hour's amusement, after our party had taken down the intermediate fences, which were too high to clear, to gallop over the whole battle-ground, and survey it from every point. A prettier spot to fight on never greeted the eye of a soldier. The undulations of the field are just sufficient to exercise a nice military discrimination in the choice of position, while the ground is yet so little broken that cavalry might act on any part of it to advantage. The centre of the battle-field would command a fine view of the river, were but a vista or two cut in the wood below; and even now it offers a beautiful site for a private residence, and would, with the lands adjacent, make a noble park. There are a few superb oaks still standing at the foot of the slope, which might constitute a lawn, and—what must enhance the value of the place with all faithful ghost-believers and pious lovers of the marvellous—the dim form of the red savage, with the ghastly spectre of his pallid victim shrinking before it, it is said, may be seen gliding at times among these hoary trunks. The exorcising light of noon most perversely shone down among them while I lingered near the spot, but I could fancy that the November wind which sighed among their branches was charged at times with a wailing sound, such—such in fact as an orthodox tree in a perfect state of health would never make of its own accord.

Returning home, one of the party proposed stopping at a gentleman's house in the vicinity, where a number of articles picked up from the field were said to be collected. Not a soul of us knew the proprietor of the establishment, and it would have amused you to see the effect produced upon its inmates,—whom I soon ascertained to be a large collection of boarding-school young ladies,— by our formidable descent upon the premises. We were asked into a handsome parlour, and in about fifteen minutes our host appeared. A gentleman of our number, whose western frankness of manner made him the most suitable spokesman at such an awkward meeting, opened the preliminaries, and apologizing for our unceremonious intrusion, revealed our character as relic hunters. The stranger host, overlooking the absence of "sandal shoon and scallop shell," welcomed us at once with the same politeness that pilgrims have ever received in civilized countries, and regretting that he had not even a remnant to swear by—not an atom of a relic—sent us home to our supper with appetites considerably sharpened by the disappointment.

Returning, I diverged with one of the company from the direct road a little, to take a look at the United States' arsenal. It lies on the banks of the Alleghany, and consists, together with the officers' quarters, of a number of handsome brick-buildings, painted cream colour, and so arranged with regard to each other as that, in connection with the improved grounds adjacent, they make quite a handsome appearance.

It was nearly dark when we got fairly into town, where the dust and smoke, with the rattling of drays along the streets, returning from their day's work to the suburbs, reminded me not a little of my own bustling city at night-fall. There is one sound, however, in the streets of Pittsburg which utterly forbids a stranger mistaking them for those of any other town on the continent—it is the ceaseless din of the steam-engines. Every mechanic here, of any pretension, has one of these tremendous journeymen at work in his establishment. They may be purchased for what would be the price of a pair of horses in New-York; and it costs a mere trifle to keep them in fuel. These machines must do the work of a great many thousand men at Pittsburg; and though I am hardly such a friend of universal suffrage as to think that these substitutes for men ought to be represented in the legislature, yet, upon my word, they should always be taken into consideration when estimating the population of the place, which their industrious labour renders so flourishing.

"Proud deeds these *iron-men* have done."

LETTER VIII.

There is no place in the Western country, as Judge Baldwin observed, in his address before the Mechanics' Institution of Pittsburg, "which can more justly boast of its small beginnings, its rapid but solid growth, and its future greatness," than this. It is about seventy years since General Washington, then a young man of two-and-twenty, was despatched by Governor Dinwiddie of Virginia to the French commander on Le Bœuf (near Erie), to demand that he should desist from aggression upon the British frontier. The young officer, on his return down the Alleghany, upon a raft made with tomahawks, was wrecked with a single Indian attendant, on an island near the present city of Pittsburg. The situation of the point of land formed by " the forks of the Ohio" at once caught his military eye; and crossing on the ice in the morning, he examined the position with sufficient minuteness to impress his commander with its importance. The spot was soon after taken possession of by a small colonial force, which in 1754 was easily dispersed by the formidable descent of the French under Contrecœur. He came with a thousand men at his back, and floated various munitions of war, among which were eighteen pieces of cannon, in three hundred and sixty canoes, down the Alleghany. The first blow was struck of the old French war, which lost France all her possessions east of the Mississippi. Contrecœur intrenched himself upon the spot, and the bloody annals of Fort *Du Quesne* received their first notoriety from this bold invader.

Thirty years afterward the place, now become known as Fort Pitt began to assume commercial importance from the Indian fur-trade then carried on with vigour from this point. An increase of population ensued; the extensive coal-beds in the vicinity began to be appreciated; they indicated the prodigious manufacturing resources of the rising town of Pittsburg. The adjacent country became rapidly peopled, and it was soon the agricultural depot for the rich region on this side of the Alleghanies. The genius of Fulton matured at once the rising fortunes of Pittsburg, and gave her a market for her overflowing productions.

Situated two thousand miles from New-Orleans, by the aid of steam she supplies the whole of the intermediate region with hardware, machinery, and cutlery.* But it is not for this manufacture alone that Pittsburg, though often called the "Birmingham of America," is celebrated. Her extensive glass-works are well known even beyond the Alleghanies ; and this fragile production of her workshops finds its way alike to the borders of Lake Erie and of the Atlantic, and may be met in the elegant mansions of Baltimore and the remote shantees of the Arkansaw.

The timber-trade is another great feature in the business relations of Pittsburg ; the boards and scantling measured within the city in **1830** amounted to more than five millions of feet ; of this a great deal was floated down the branches of the Alleghany River from the south-western counties of New-York. The romantic hills of Chatauque county supply not a few of the stately trunks which, after being hewn into shape at Pittsburg, subsequently float the varied products of Northern industry through many a stranger cli-

* Bloom-iron, I am told, is brought hither for manufacture from the forges on the Juniata, from Tennessee, Kentucky, and Missouri ; and contracts are frequently made for $38 per ton to take the blooms at St. Louis, and return them rolled iron.

mate to the rich markets of Louisiana. You will
not wonder, therefore, that the freight exported
from Pittsburg in 1830 amounted to upwards of
18,000 tons, its imports for the same year being
more than 14,000 tons. The city is now, with the
adjacent villages of Alleghany-town and Lawrence-
ville on the Alleghany, and Birmingham and Man-
chester on the Monongahela, the third town in population, wealth, and importance in the Mississippi
valley. Next to its admirable situation, the flourishing condition of the place is no doubt to be mainly
attributed to the inexhaustible quantities of fine
bituminous coal which may be had for the digging
in all the adjacent hills. Pittsburg is, however,
indebted to the character of her early settlers for
her present eminence; they were chiefly mechanics, enterprising, industrious, practical men;
the improvements they commenced were based
upon utility, and every path of trade they struck
out led to some immediate and tangible good. The
result shows itself in one of the most substantial
and flourishing, but least elegant, cities on the continent. The site of the town I have already described to you as one of the most beautiful that can
be imagined. The want of beauty in the place
itself is to be attributed entirely to the manner in
which it is laid out, for the streets, though by no

means wide, are well and substantially built upon
with brick; and a species of yellow freestone found
in the vicinity is coming into use, which, for elegance as a building-material, is not surpassed by
marble itself. The great defect in the town is the
total want of public squares, and, indeed, of an
agreeable promenade of any kind; this is the more
remarkable, I might almost say provoking, as Pittsburg boasts of one spot which, if converted into a
public place, would, from the view it commands,
be unrivalled by any thing of the kind in the
Union, unless it be the Battery of New-York. I
allude to a triangular piece of ground, at the con-
fluence of the two rivers, at the end of the town.
It is the site of the old forts, and commands the
first view of the Ohio, and the finest of its waters
I have yet seen; the prospect I have described to
you in a former letter. Had but the ancient fortifi-
cations been preserved, this would have been one
of the most interesting spots upon the continent; of
Fort Du Quesne there remains now but a small
mound, containing, perhaps, a couple of loads of
earth; Fort Pitt may be more easily traced, part
of three bastions, about breast-high, stand within
different private enclosures, and a piece of the
curtain, which, within a few years, was in complete
preservation, may still be discovered among the

piles of lumber in a steam saw-mill yard. The commandant's quarters, a steep-roofed brick dwelling, in the form of a pentagon, is, however, the only perfect remnant of these old military structures. I expected to have seen the magazine of the fort, which I was told was an admirable piece of masonry, and still endured in the shape of a porter-cellar; but upon arriving at the spot where it had stood but a few weeks before, a pile of rough stones was all that we could discover. In a country like ours, where so few antiquities meet the eye, it is melancholy to see these interesting remnants thus destroyed, and the very landmarks where they stood effaced for ever. Occasionally, too, the works of which every vestige is thus painfully obliterated were, especially when erected by the French, of a peculiarly striking character. The French engineers, who first introduced the art of fortification into this country, were of the school of Vauban, and the enduring monuments they raised were not less noble proofs of their skill than were the sites selected of their high military discernment.

There is yet another place in Pittsburg which at some future day should be appropriated as a public square; a triangular bluff about one hundred feet high stretches like a huge promontory

far into the town, and overlooks the whole place.
The Pittsburgers, however, I fear, are more bent
upon increasing their "fathers' store" than on
beautifying the favoured spot in which they dwell;
and it requires all the cordial hospitality of the
place to reconcile a stranger to the few city improvements he sees going forward, in a community
so pre-eminent for its individual enterprise.   I
wish we could lend them our "improving" corporation for a few weeks,—they would be really of
service here, and could easily be spared at home;
they might, too, learn more than one thing of the
Pittsburgers, and especially how to supply the
city with pure water; we have it here in the
greatest abundance.   The water is pumped up
from the Alleghany by a steam-engine, into a large
open basin, situated on an eminence known as
Grant's Hill, from the signal defeat of that rash but
gallant officer at its base, during the old French
war.   From this ample reservoir pipes conduct
the fluid to every part of the city.   A large Gothic
cathedral is now about to be erected near the
water-works.

You remember Grant's fight, as described by
Hall, in his beautiful Western Sketches.   Grant
bivouacked beneath the hill now called after him,
and ordering his reveille to beat at dawn; the

French and Indians charged upon him to the sound of his own trumpets, and cut his troops to pieces. His force, I believe, consisted chiefly of Highlanders. The skeleton of a young officer, with gold in his pocket and marks of rank about his person, was turned up in a field not far distant, a few years since. A western poet, of whose existence I first became aware through a file of the Pittsburg Gazette (for the use of which, with many interesting facts relating to the adjacent country, I am indebted to the politeness of Mr. Craig, the editor), has commemorated the incident in some verses, among which are the following simple lines :—

> " One Highland officer that bloody day
>   Retreated up the Alleghany side ;
>   Wounded and faint, he missed his tangled way,
>   And near its waters laid him down and died.
>
> 'Twas in a furrow of a sandy swell
>   Which overlooks the clear and pebbled wave ;
>   Shrouded in leaves, none found him where he fell,
>   And mouldering nature gave the youth a grave.
>
> Last year a plough passed o'er the quiet spot,
>   And brought to light frail vestiges of him,
>   Whose unknown fate perhaps is not forgot,
>   And fills with horror yet a sister's dream."

On the side of the hill is a place still pointed out as " Grant's grave." I know not why it should be thus designated, however ; for I believe that the worthy colonel, who afterward served in the British army during the Revolution, never returned to lay his bones in a spot where the spirits of his rashly sacrificed soldiers might have made him uneasy in his grave. There is a more authentic tomb on the western bank of the Alleghany : it is the last resting-place of an Indian, who, as tradition avers, seeing " Helen's beauty in a brow of Egypt," shot himself for love !—an instance of intense regard—of passionate devotion to woman which most writers upon Indian character would have us believe could never exhibit itself in

" The stoic of the woods."

The walks and rides in the environs of Pittsburg are rendered interesting by a variety of objects, besides the fine scenery through which they lead. A description of the Pennsylvania Canal, which flows on an aqueduct over the Alleghany, and passing through a tunnel of a few yards in length, locks into the Monongahela, on the opposite side of the city, would furnish you with no newer ideas than a description of any other canal. The Nunnery, which is also one of the lions of the neighbourhood, I have not hitherto had an oppor-

tunity to visit, and "Braddock's field" you have
already in a letter by itself; so, having now a tolerable idea of the town—with its compact brick
dwellings, dingy with coal-smoke; its natural
wharves, where the Ohio rises 25 feet; its gravelly
banks, lined with steamboats and river-craft, and
bustling with business operations upon the most
extensive scale—you must follow me in my ride of
this morning along the Monongahela.

The fog and coal-smoke together rendered the
atmosphere so thick, even after crossing the bridge
over the river to a straggling village opposite, that
I verily believe it was only the dazzling sparkle of
a pair of queen-like eyes, marshalling me through
the gloom, that enabled me to ascend the opposite
height with safety. Leaving the rest of the party
far behind, I followed their beautiful and high-
spirited owner up a windng path, where our horses,
after sinking to their fetlocks in the clayey soil,
would slip half a pace backward at every step, and
gained at last an elevation nearly five hundred feet
above the level of the river, where, to my surprise,
instead of a sudden descent upon the opposite side,
the eminence continued rising. in a succession of
fertile fields, until the last green slope was terminated by a distant wood. We rode along the
edge of the precipice for a mile or two, and from

the state of the atmosphere on the side towards the town, you can conceive nothing more singular than the effect of the scene below. Imagine yourself standing on Weehawk Height, with your own city brought immediately beneath your feet, the whole landscape bright and clear above, and a cloud so impervious below that not an object can be discerned at five yards' distance. The gulf seems unfathomable. The hoarse jar of machinery comes upon the ear like the groans of a nether world; and the lurid flame which ever and anon shoots from some furnace athwart the gloom shows like the penal element itself. But now the noonday sun has pierced into that murky glen,—the fog begins to rise,—a gilded spire glances here and there in the broad sunshine, and some tall headland stands greenly out from the silver veil that wraps its base; the banner from yonder arsenal floats gayly forth in the warm air; and as the flaky mist rolls more rapidly up the river, begins to stream upon the freshening breeze. The rivers themselves can now be traced far away, with many a dewy island stealing out, one by one, upon their bosom. Beneath, a bustling city seems as if it had sprung at once to life, while the quiet farmhouses slowly appear upon the sleeping fields beyond.

This single view is worth a journey to Pittsburg.

I took an opportunity, while a lady of the party stopped to visit a pensioner in a cottage by the road-side, to examine a coal-pit just beneath the brow of the hill. Dismounting on a small platform some two hundred feet above the river, from which a railway empties the coal into the *coke*-kilns upon its bank and the freight-boats upon the shore, I entered an aperture in the rock, about six feet in height and four in breadth. A guide preceded me with a candle, and after penetrating under his escort a few hundred yards, I turned aside to explore some of the adjacent shafts: they lie like the streets of one main avenue,—the veins of a grand artery, which, after winding through the body of the hill, for the distance of half a mile, finds its way again to the light. In one of these cavernous passages, in a ledge of the rock, lay a sleeping man, the water trickling from the black walls around was the only sound to disturb his slumbers; a long-wicked candle stuck in a crevice above his head, shining over thickly-matted locks, and features begrimmed with coal-dust, revealed a figure of gigantic mould. The mattock on which his ponderous arm reposed told that it was only a miner at his noonday nap; but he might have been mistaken, by one coming suddenly upon his singular place of repose, for a slumbering Titan, who, though pent within such narrow confines, might yet shake the mountain piled upon him to its base.

Our route now, after leading still farther along the height, commanding at every step some new view of the town and the adjacent country, with the three rivers seaming its bosom, struck at last into a fine wood, and then descending suddenly into a romantic dell, followed a small stream which soon led us back to the Ohio. Here, again, might be traced a display of French taste, which, when the fabric was entire, must have been exceedingly beautiful. It was the remains of a mill-dam constructed by the officers of Fort Du Quesne, according to the most approved rules of the time, like a perfect fortification ; a part of the curtain, with traces of some of the bastions, yet reward the eye of the curious. At the mouth of the glen we paused to look at a salt factory ; and then crossing a bridge over the brook, we passed by a steel factory, and several coke-kilns, situated along the base of the cliff, from the summit of which I had recently looked down upon and admired the scene below.

The embouchure of the Monongahela was at hand, and stepping on board of a small horse-boat at the point where that river loses itself in the Ohio, I soon terminated on the opposite side one of the most delightful rides I can recollect to have taken.

LETTER IX.

Cleaveland, Ohio, Nov. 15.

I took my passage in the stage-coach for this place early in the evening three days since, and having at a late hour bade adieu to more than one whose friendship I trust will not be the less enduring that it was made in so brief a space of time, retired to my chamber to catch a nap before my morning's ride. The clock was striking three, when at the call of the porter I rose and descended to the bar-room. The attentive landlord, himself in waiting, was ruminating before a large coal-fire; and stretched upon the floor in a corner lay the tired domestic, who, having just fulfilled a part of his duty, in awakening the various passengers, was catching a dog-nap before the stage-coach should drive to the door. The flavour of last night's potations still hung around the scene of so many symposia, and the fragrance of more than one recently smoked segar stole, charged with the aroma of whiskey, upon the senses. Cold as it was, I was not sorry to snuff a less scented atmosphere, as each stage that passed the house in succession hurried me vainly to the door. My own proper vehicle came at last, and by the light of the stage lamps,—the only ones, by-the-by, which shone through the sleeping city,—I climbed to the coachman's box, and took the traveller's favourite seat by his side. It was as dark as Erebus when we crossed the bridge over the Alleghany, and looking back when we had passed the gate and were turning into the village, I could distinguish nothing of the city opposite but the red glare of a furnace which shot out from the bank of the river, and glowed an inverted pyramid of light upon its waters. Keeping on our way, the massive walls of the state-prison, with their circular towers and octangular area, frowned like some old Moorish castle over our path, as we drove beneath their dun-coloured battlements, and passed the last environs of Pittsburg. It was, I confess, with some soberness of spirit that I bade a last adieu to a spot where the politeness and hospitality of the inhabitants had made my time pass so pleasantly. I must, however, have been *de trop* among my new acquaintances, had I remained much longer: for in Pittsburg every one is so occupied with business, that the time bestowed in attentions to a stranger is a sacrifice of some importance. I have since been much vexed to find, in looking over my papers here, that a letter of introduction, from a most flattering source, to the U. S. officer now commanding at Pittsburg, escaped me entirely. I was chagrined the more, inasmuch as I should have liked both to visit the arsenal, and to make the acquaintance of the valued officer who has charge of it. I had not, however, this reflection to annoy me as, wrapped up warmly, I rode along, watching the cheerful dawn, streaking the east with pencillings of light, and dappling with ruddy rays the broad bosom of the Ohio. As the morning gradually broke, I discovered that the banks of the river presented a different appearance from what they did when I sailed along them ten days before. The November winds had been at work in the woods. The gorgeous panoply of autumn no longer hung on the forest. The trees stood bare in the growing sunlight, and the thick-strewn leaves rustled to the tread of the gray squirrel that leaped from the naked boughs by the roadside.

We stopped to breakfast at a low log-built shantee, within a stone's throw of the river, and being asked into a narrow chamber, half-parlour, half-kitchen, I had for the first time an opportunity, as we collected around the breakfast table, to survey my fellow-passengers. They were chiefly plain people, small farmers and graziers, returning perhaps from market, where they had been to part with their produce. Their manner, like most of our countrymen of the same class, was grave and decorous at table, to a degree approaching to solemnity, though they ate with the rapidity characteristic of Americans at their meals. The ceremony of the board commenced by the oldest man in the company taking a beef-steak before him, and cutting it into small pieces with his own knife and fork. He then passed the dish around to each, and finally, when all were served, helped himself. The bread was in the same way circulated by the youngest of the company, and then, each having as fair a start as his neighbour, we all fell to work with a lustihood that would have done beef-eating Queen Bess good to witness. The appetites of those present were generally sharpened by the morning's ride ; and, maugre the huge piles of buckwheat-cakes that smoked along the board flanked each by a cold apple-pie, the beef-steak was decidedly the favourite dish ; and was meted out again and again, by the same knife and fork that played a private part the whiles for the stout yeoman who thus plied them for the public good. Your bandbox-bred *elegant,* who was ignorant that the Spaniards and the Turks, the two most polite peoples in the world, thrust their fingers into the reeking bowl of olla podrida, or the smoking dish of pilau—while, like our sturdy Pennsylvanian, they always help their fellow-travellers of the caravanserai, or posada, before attending to themselves —might have turned up his nose in a transport of Trollopism at such refinement. The charge of vulgarity, however, would rest only with him who, mistaking the conventional rules of society for the essential principles of politeness, should measure the manners of strangers by the standard of his own narrow circle. There was but one of my fellow-passengers I observed, who ate with his fork. He was better dressed, and sat somewhat apart from the rest, interchanging with them none of the homely but hearty civilities which they proffered to each other. I set him down as some Eastern shop-keeper, who, though he might have been envied by a Chinese for the chop-stick dexterity with which he managed to pitch the morsels of food into his mouth with a two-pronged fork, might better have passed the time spent in acquiring his sleight-of-hand in gaining real good-breeding, from those whom he evidently set down in his own mind as far beneath him.

Pursuing our journey, we stopped soon after to

change horses at *Economy*. I was much disappointed in not having even five minutes to look through this celebrated village, where the German Rapp has so successfully raised a community, who labour in common, and own all their property only as trust members of a corporation. I saw hardly as much of the town, thus passing its suburbs inland, as when sailing by the front on the Ohio. It struck me as remarkably neat, however; and it being Sunday, a perfect silence seemed to reign over the village. Rapp, I believe, unlike most of his co-community-mongers, retains religion, not only as incident to, but an essential feature of, his system. Had it been otherwise, the attempt to form such an establishment could hardly have succeeded as it has. Religion I believe to be an instinct of the human mind—a natural impulse, which at some time determines the thoughts of every heart heavenward. It is a feeling which as palpably prompts us to seek a God and to worship him, as does the instinct of a bird suggest the season of building her nest and the materials for its construction. The form of her frail fabric varies indeed with the climate in which it is built, and the character of the winged artificer: but the haughty temples of heathenism, the sumptuous mosques of the Mussulman, and the Christian's humbler house of worship may each find a semblance on the towering cliffs or tall tree-top, where birds of prey alone will build,—in the imbowered copse, where the luxurious dove delights to brood,—or mid the lowly rushes, where the lapwing's fragile nest is made. There is, indeed, a stolid race of birds who deposite their eggs upon the barren shore, leaving the sun to vivify or the sea to scatter their contents as chance may determine. But stupid as their offspring must he be who, in constructing an aviary, made no provision for the interesting wants of the rest of the species, because this particular genus is so coarsely constituted. Let us thank Heaven, when thinking of the privileges of which the intrusive bigotry of foreign infidels at times would strip us, that in our free forests, there are fields, hills, and groves where religion, unshackled as a new-fledged bird, may build her altars how and where she pleases.

Our route continuing along the river, we soon passed a fine elevated field on the bank where General Wayne—or Mad Antony, as he was more familiarly called—encamped with his army that encountered the Indians so successfully near the Miami of the Lakes.

The stone fireplaces of the soldiery, now overgrown with turf, were, with a few other scattered marks of the encampment, discernible upon the ground; and they suggested to one of the passengers the well-known anecdote of the general having one of his men tried and shot for desertion, because he had, without permission from his officer, accompanied an only brother, his visiter at the camp, a few miles on his return home. The example was a terrible one, but the condition of Wayne's army, from which the men were daily dropping off, strongly required it; and I confess that in military affairs I respect the firmness equal to such an occasion too much to merge my admiration of the unblenching disciplinarian in sympathy for the unfortunate sufferer.

We reached the thriving town of Beaver about noon, and crossing the creek of the same name by a high wooden bridge, struck inland, and soon lost sight of the beautiful Ohio in the broken country that here approaches its banks. A cold shower drove me for protection inside the stage, and there, wrapping myself up as comfortably as I could, I passed the night. The passengers had gradually dropped off along the road, leaving only a solitary country merchant and myself. We beguiled the time for a while in conversation, and then, as midnight came on, and he grew drowsy, I resigned myself to the same influence that had begun to send sounds any thing but musical from his "innocent nose." Awaking with the sun, I found that we were in the midst of new clearings, the road leading through a level country as far as the eye could reach, and having its sides faced beyond the fields with trees, which, with tall stems and interlacing summits, stood like giants locking arms along the highway. I must now be in Ohio, thought I; and I was right. The effect of this magnificent vegetation was striking even at this season; but after riding for half a day along such a wood, with not a valley to break the view, nor a hill to bound it, it could not but be monotonous. We passed two lakes in the course of our ride, approaching one of them near enough to see that it was a clear sheet of water, with a pretty yellow sand-beach. But, though shut up by woods, it wanted entirely the wild yet gentle picturesqueness of the lakes I have seen among and near the Highlands of the Hudson; much less could it boast of the savage grandeur of those which form the sources of that princely river.

The most interesting objects on this route are decidedly the growing towns and hamlets which abound along the road. Some of them have been manufactured only this season; and it is really surprising to see rude log huts of two years' date standing side by side with tasteful edifices of yesterday, like the old and new branches of one flourishing tree; brick churches and hotels, with handsome porticoes, surrounded by the stumps of recently-felled forests. In one village, called Hudson, particularly,—where, by-the-way, much good taste is exhibited in the private houses, —the progress of improvement is said to be as perceptible as the rise of the tide at the seaboard. I could not, however, discover a palpable growth in the place from the time we sat down to dinner till hurried away from table by the call of the stage-driver.

We reached Cleaveland during a heavy shower long after nightfall. The roar of the surf reminded me of Rockaway; and the first view of Lake Erie, the next morning, was really grateful to my eyes. I felt, while walking along the high esplanade of turf which here forms its banks, and upon which the town is built, like one who has just come out of a pent-up chamber into the full and free air of heaven. The effect of coming on such a wide expanse of water when just emerging from the forest is much greater than when, after long riding through an open country, you view the ocean stretched beyond its shining beach.

Cleaveland is very prettily situated upon the lake. The Cayuhoga makes a bend around a high bluff as it passes into the inland sea which receives its waters, and on the level peninsula thus formed is built the town. The harbour, naturally an indifferent one, has been much improved by running out a pier from either side of the river, where it debouches into Lake Erie; and there being now few better ports on this side of the lake, Cleaveland must become one of the most important places on its waters. The adjacent region is, I believe, not remarkably well suited to agricultural purposes; but there is an immense tract of the most fertile country inland, which looks to Cleaveland for the chief outlet of its products. This will account for the rapid rise of property here, which is almost incredible; building-lots in some places commanding now as many thousands as they did hundreds of dollars five years since. The town, which can already boast of a public library, a fine church, two capital taverns, and many handsome private dwellings, is laid out with broad streets and a spacious square in the centre. The business part is as yet beneath the bluff, where a single winding street runs along the bank of the river towards the lake; but the main street above is already the scene of much bustle, and bears about the same relation to that below as Broadway does to South-street in your city.

I have been happy here to meet with some old school-fellows settled in the place—where, indeed, among our wandering people can one tread without finding an acquaintance?—and this morning I was agreeably surprised by finding an English groom waiting at the door for me with a fine saddle-horse, and mentioning that my friend its owner would soon join me with another. We first rode out through a clearing, back of the village, and enjoyed a very pretty prospect of the Cayuhoga winding through a piece of rich meadow-land below us, and affording, as the high grounds recede at its entrance into the lake, a striking view of Erie in the distance. Returning upon our tracks, we passed the village on the east, and then rode westwardly along the shore of the lake. The banks, which are high and covered with sod on the top, are here composed of clay and gravel: on the surface they appear perfectly firm, but for the distance of nearly a mile along shore they have sunk, or are sinking, to the breadth of about 300 feet, and slipped off into the lake, whose waters thus swallow building-lots worth a great amount of money. The cause is believed to lie in quicksands beneath; and it offers a singular phenomenon to stand on the shore below, and marking the sunken platforms of earth behind, see where half an acre of clay has risen through the sandy beach in front, within a few inches of the surface of the water.

The treacherous attributes of the shore suggested to my companion, who, though young, has been a traveller in his day, an incident he witnessed while journeying through some of the remote provinces of Mexico, which would make no feeble subject for the pencil of Weir or Inman. He had ridden with an English gentleman for many hours through an unsettled country, where not a drop of water was to be obtained for their horses, when, coming suddenly upon a clear stream, sparkling over its bed of yellow sand, their weary beasts sprang forward simultaneously, to drink from the grateful current. A break in the bank caused their riders to rein up and dismount, retaining at the same time the loosened reins in their hands, while their horses stepped down to the margin of the brook. The American, finding that the deceitful bottom yielded as soon as touched, jerked his terrified beast from the fatal spot, while as yet his forefeet were only immersed in the quicksand. But the horse of the Englishman, in his eagerness to get at the water, made but one step to destruction. He sunk floundering to his shoulders before an effort could be made to rescue him ; and then, as in his struggles to extricate himself from the ingulfing pool, he heaved his broad chest high above its surface, and the sucking sands drew his quarters in a moment beneath them. The nostrils of the suffering animal dilated with the fierce death encounter, and giving that hideous cry—

" The cry of steeds that shriek in agony,"

he tossed his head frantically above his greedy grave—his mane fluttered for a moment on the shallow water, and the bed of the stream closed over him for ever.

LETTER X.

Detroit, Michigan, November 25.

I had just left the reading-room of the Franklin Hotel, in Cleaveland, and was making myself at home for the rest of the evening, in my own neat chamber, when the sound of a steamboat-bell, about nine o'clock, gave note that one of these vessels, which at this stormy season cannot navigate the lake with any regularity, had touched at Cleaveland on her way to this place. No time was to be lost, and huddling my clothes, &c. into my trunk as quickly as possible, I jumped into a vehicle, waiting at the tavern door, and in a few minutes was upon the quay. Here I witnessed a scene of indescribable confusion. The night was dark and somewhat gusty, and the boat and the wharf were both crowded with boxes, bales, and the effects of emigrants, who were screaming to each other in half as many languages as were spoken at Babel. Lanterns were flashing to and fro along the docks, and hoarse orders and countermands, mingled with the harsh hissing of the steam on every side. At length we pushed from the shore, and escaping in a moment from the head of the mole, stood fairly out into the lake, while the bright beacon of the Cleaveland lighthouse soon waned in the distance, and was at last lost entirely. I found myself, upon looking around, on board of the fine steamboat "New-York," Captain Fisher, to whose politeness I was much indebted for showing me about the boat before turning in for the night. Taking a lantern in his hand, and tucking my arm under his, he groped about among his motley ship's company like Diogenes looking for an honest man.

Our course first led us through a group of emigrants collected around a stove, mid-ships, where an English mother nursing her infant, a child lying asleep upon a mastiff, and a long-bearded German smoking his meerchaum on the top of a pile of candle-boxes, were the only complete figures I could make out from an indefinite number of heads, arms, and legs lying about in the most whimsical confusion. Passing farther on, we came to two tolerable cabins on either side of the boat just forward of the wheels, both pretty well filled with emigrants, who were here more comfortably bestowed. We next passed the forward bar-room (there being another abaft for cabin-passengers), and finally came to the bow, of which a horse and several dogs had already been the occupants for so many days,—the New-York having been twice driven into port and delayed by stress of weather, —that it might have been mistaken for either stable or kennel. A noble English blood-hound, the second dog only of that rare breed that I have ever seen, here attracted my attention, and delayed me until I made his acquaintance; which was but a moment, however, for every dog of a generous strain can tell instinctively when a friend of his kind approaches him.

Among others of the canine crew, too, there was a fine spaniel, whose deplorable fate, subsequently, I may as well mention here as elsewhere. The master of poor Dash, it seems, went ashore during the night at Huron, where the boat put in to land way-passengers; and the animal, springing eagerly along a plank at his call, was kicked from his narrow foothold, by some brute of a fellow, into the lake. The night was dark, and the shadow of the high wharf shut out the few lights on shore from the view of the poor animal, while those on board of the boat led him away from the land. He swam after us, yelling most piteously, until his suffocating cries were lost in the freshening sea, which probably the next morning tossed him a carrion on the shore. Had I witnessed the act of throwing him overboard, I could scarcely have restrained myself from pitching the dastardly perpetrator of the cruelty after the victim of his brutality: for if there be one trait in men which awakens in me indignation amounting almost to loathing of my kind, it is to see human things treating those parts of the animal creation beneath them as if this earth was meant for none of God's creatures but man.

But to return to our travels through this floating castle: We next ascended a steep stairway to the upper deck of all, and I here spent some moments rather amusingly in surveying the furniture of the emigrants with which it was crowded. They differed according to the origin of their owner. The effects of the Yankee were generally limited to a Dearborn wagon, a feather-bed, a saddle and bridle, and some knickknack in the way of a machine for shelling corn, hatchelling flax, or, for aught I know, manufacturing wooden nutmegs for family use. Those of the Englishman are far more numerous; for John Bull, when he wanders from home, would not only, like the roving

Trojan, carry his household gods with him into strange lands, but even the fast-anchored isle itself, could he but cut it from its moorings. Whenever, therefore, you see an antique-fashioned looking-glass, a decrepit bureau, and some tenderly-preserved old china, you will probably, upon looking further, have the whole house-keeping array of an honest Briton exposed to your view.

But still further do the Swiss and Germans carry their love of family relics. Mark that quaint-looking wagon which lumbers up a dozen square feet of the deck. You may see a portrait of it among the illuminated letters of a vellum-bound edition of Virgil's Bucolics. It was taken from an Helvetian ancestor that transported Cæsar's baggage into winter-quarters. It might be worth something in a museum, but it has cost five times its value in freight to transport it over the Atlantic. What an indignity it is to overwhelm the triumphal chariot with the beds and ploughs, shovels, saddles, and sideboards, chairs, clocks, and carpets that fill its interior, and to hang those rusty pots and kettles, bakepans, fryingpans, and saucepans, iron candlesticks, old horse-shoes, and broken tobacco-pipes, like trophies of conquest over Time, along its racked and wheezing sides. That short man yonder, with square shoulders and a crooked pipe in his mouth, is the owner; he, with the woollen cap, that is just raising his blue cotton frock to thrust his hand into the fob of his sherrivalleys. That man had probably not the slightest idea of the kind of country he was coming to. His eyes are but now just opening to his new condition; nor will he sacrifice a particle of his useless and expensive trumpery until they are completely open. That man has not yet a thought in common with the people of his new abode around him. He looks, indeed, as if he came from another planet. Visit him on his thriving farm ten years hence, and, except in the single point of language, you will find him (unless he has settled among a nest of his countrymen) at home among his neighbours, and happily conforming to their usages; while that clean-looking Englishman next to him will still be a stranger in the land.

I subsequently looked into the different cabins and compartments of the boat not yet visited, and had reason to be gratified with the appearance of all; though the steamboat Michigan, which I have since visited at the docks here, puts me completely out of conceit of every part of the New-York, except her captain. The Michigan, machinery and all, was built at Detroit; and without entering into a minute description of it, I may say, that fine as our Atlantic boats are, I do not recollect any on the Atlantic waters, for strength and beauty united, equal to this. A great mistake, however, I think, exists here in building the boats for these waters with cabins on deck, like the river boats. In consequence of such a large part of the hull being above water, they are rendered dangerous during the tremendous gales which sweep Lake Erie, and are often compelled to make a port of safety several times during a passage. The English steamers which ply between Dover and Calais are built like other sea-vessels; and having their machinery below, can consequently keep on their course in a sea where one of ours would live but a few minutes. I was fortunate, considering the stormy season of the year, in having a tolerably smooth passage across the lake, there being but few persons sea-sick on board of the boat, and I happily not included in the number. But it must be very unpleasant, during a heavy blow, to be tossed on the short cobble sea which the light fresh water of these lakes always breaks into beneath the wind.

We passed a number of islands in the morning soon after breakfast; some of them mere rocks, and others several miles in circumference. On one of these, of a few acres in extent, a row-boat, in which a man undertook to transport himself and one or two members of his family to the shore, was wrecked some years since. The father and brother, with a daughter of about twelve years, managed to subsist upon the snakes and snails they found among the rocks, until a passing vessel took them off, after some ten days of suffering.

It was during a shower, shortly after noon, when some low wooded islands on the American side of the lake, with a tall flag-staff peering above the haze from the little town of Amherstburg on the British shore, indicated that we had entered the mouth of the Detroit River. The wind, which was now beginning to rise into a threatening tempest, compelled us to hug the Canadian shore so closely, that the red-coated sentinel pacing along the barracks above Fort Malden was plainly seen from the boat. The river soon after narrows sufficiently for one to mark with ease the general appearance of its banks, and the different settlements upon their course. Their appearance must be pretty in summer, when fields and woods show to the most advantage. But now, though slightly undulating, with a sudden rise from the river of some fifty or sixty feet, the adjacent country is too low to be strikingly beautiful. Those, however, who admire the Delaware below Trenton, if they can dispense with the handsome seats which ornament its not very clear waters, may find a charm in the gentle banks and transparent tide of the Detroit River.

The city of Detroit itself stands upon an elevated piece of table-land, extending probably for some twenty miles back from the river, and being perfectly unbroken for at least two miles along its margin. Beneath the bluff—for the plain is so high as almost to deserve the name—is a narrow bustling street of about half a mile in length, with the wharves just beyond it; and fifty yards inboard runs a spacious street called Jefferson Avenue, parallel with the lower street and the river; the chief part of the town extends for a mile or two along the latter. The dwelling-houses are generally of wood, but there are a great many stores now building, or already erected, of brick, with stone basements. The brick is generally of an indifferent quality; but the stone, which is brought from Cleaveland, Ohio, is a remarkably fine material for building purposes. It is a kind of yellow freestone, which is easily worked when first taken from the quarry, and hardens subsequently upon exposure to the air. There are at this moment many four-story stores erecting, as well as other substantial buildings, which speak for the flourishing condition of the place.

The want of mechanics is so great, however, that it is difficult as yet to carry on these operations upon the scale common in our Atlantic cities, although the demand for houses in Detroit, it is said, would fully warrant similar outlays of capital. The public buildings are the territorial council-house, situated upon an open piece of ground, designated on an engraved plan of the city as "The Campus Martius," a court-house, academy, and two banks. There are also five churches, a Catholic, an Episcopal, a Presbyterian, Baptist, and Methodist. The Catholic congregation is the largest; their stone church, after remaining several years in an unfinished state, is soon, it is said, to be completed with funds derived from Rome; it will make an imposing appearance when finished. The population of Detroit is, I believe, between three and four thousand—it increases so rapidly, however, that it is difficult to form an estimate. The historical associations, the safety, and commodiousness of the harbour, with its extensive inland commercial advantages, must ever constitute this one of the most interesting and important points in the Union, although other causes may combine to make newer places in the territory equally as flourishing as Detroit.

The appearance of the place is any thing but what you would expect from a town founded in the same year with Philadelphia. The ancient houses, which formerly stood upon streets hardly ten feet wide, were all swept away in the great fire twenty years since, and the new white dwellings, standing upon broad avenues of twenty-five yards, make the town look like a place of yesterday.

I am surprised to find but few military remains in a frontier post so frequently fortified, and which has witnessed so many scenes of border war. A small stone arsenal, with a tall picket fence around it, is the only thing of the kind discoverable, and yet the place is thought by military men to have been sufficiently strong during the last war to have held out, if properly commanded, against twice the force which the brave General Brock brought against it. The lapse of twenty-two years has not yet cooled the indignation of the inhabitants at its dastardly surrender by Hull. It is necessary to see the ground to estimate properly that besotted act, at which his officers broke their swords, and his men nearly rose in open mutiny; while even the women of the fort shut the gates, and declared that their husbands and brothers should not abide by the disgraceful orders of their commander. It is astounding to think how slight an exertion of force might have annihilated the attacking party. They landed about two miles below the town, and advanced in solid column along a straight road, which runs parallel with the river, and is walled inland with a high picket fence, in front of the French farm-houses which line the way. At the entrance of the town, and nearly in front of the hotel where I am staying, were planted two pieces of cannon, loaded with grape and canister. A single discharge must have swept half of the British force into eternity, while the river on one side, and the high picket on the other, would have hedged the remainder in upon a spot where the destruction of the whole would have been inevitable. The artillerymen were standing with lighted portfires, when the order to retire within the fort caused them to fling their matches to the ground, and leave it with disgust. The memory of General Hull, which, with that love of glorification that constitutes the weakest point of our national character, was so hallowed in the Eastern newspapers when he died, a few years since, is here held in the contempt that was the due of a man who was sen-

tenced to be shot to death for conduct entailing so
much disgrace upon the nation.

I was not a little amused while talking over
these events, with some gentlemen a few evenings
since, upon the very scene of contention, to hear
a person, whom I soon discovered to be an Englishman, sliding into the conversation, and taking
his part of it with equal animation and good feeling ; upholding, however, like a leal and true
Briton, the acts of his own nation. The conversation was very frank on both sides, although,
when he spoke of the Kentuckians flaying the body
of Tecumseh after the battle of the Thames, I
could not trust myself to retaliate by mentioning
Proctor's massacre at Frenchtown of the flower
of the youth of Kentucky, which, as you know,
prompted this ferocious act of their countrymen,
in relation to the fierce but noble savage. The
ball of conversation, which had hitherto been
thrown with equal temper and breeding by better
and abler hands, fell into mine, just as " the delicate question of impressment" was suggested by
the English stranger ; and in begging him to dis-
miss a matter upon which our views could so little
harmonize, I could not help adding the opinion you
have often heard me express, though of course in

a manner that conveyed nothing offensive, that my country should never notice the existence of that national difficulty except through the mouths of our cannon; that is, that we should regard and treat impressment like piracy or kidnapping on the highway. "Kidnapping!" exclaimed my well-bred antagonist, smiling jocosely at the word, and politely waiving the further discussion of the subject, "why, I myself, sir, have been taken up for kidnapping within the very precincts of this town." He then went on to tell, in quite dramatic style, a series of whimsical adventures which he met with, when on a surveying party on the Lakes, just after the last war. ("Surveying on the Lakes twenty years ago!" exclaimed I to myself; "why, who can this man be? I have already travelled with him, since tea, over all Europe and a great part of Asia, not to mention the West Indies and South America, with the whole coast of Africa.") The lively and unaffected relation was every thing to the story, which at once enlisted the attention of all present, but the particulars were barely these: —The stranger, then a subaltern in the British service, was sent by his commanding officer to seize some deserters, who had escaped by night from the schooner in which the surveying-party were embarked, and which was anchored in the Detroit River. He landed on the American shore, and tracing one of the knaves to an inn hard-by, he seized him near the door, handcuffed him, and handed him to his men to take off to their boat in waiting. Then entering the inn, the sight of a number of articles stolen by the runaways induced the young officer to search for the rest of their number. Provoked at his want of success, he very naturally exclaimed, while passing vainly from room to room, " Well, thank Heaven, I have one of the rascals in limbo." A stout-looking fellow present immediately slid out of the apartment. The young Englishman, tired at last with his search of the premises, determined to leave the house to look further elsewhere. His foot was on the threshold of the door. " Stop there, you mister," exclaimed a tall Yankee, bringing a bayonet to a charge at his breast, " you don't come here and kidnap our citizens at that rate, I guess."

" Kidnap your citizens ! Why, my good fellow, that was a rascally deserter that I apprehended."

" Deserter or no deserter, we don't want no such doings over our side ; and you don't budge from here, my hearty, except to go before Governor Cass."

" Governor Cass ! Why, my dear sir, I have a

letter here for Governor Cass, and am anxious to find him out in person."

It was "no go," however, as the sturdy yeoman said, and he and his comrades at once led our young and hasty adventurer to the residence of the governor.   Detroit was then a military post of the first distinction.   The town was crowded with officers and their families, and on that very day there was a levee, at which three general officers with their respective suites received company at the governor's.   The culprit was politely received by the governor, and being soon drawn within a group of officers, they all heartily sympathized with him, and agreed that they might, without thinking, have acted similarly in violating a foreign territory when sent after "a scoundrel of a deserter."   It was, in short, a mere matter of moonshine, and the young offender need give himself no concern about it, but fill his glass, and let the hour bring forth what it might.   To make a long story short, however, our subaltern was soon ordered before the governor, who in a totally altered manner explained the grave nature of his offence to him, and told him he must be handed over to the civil authority; adding, that if he did not like to go to jail, he might take up his residence in the fort, under the care of Captain O'Fallon, whose polite-

ness the English gentleman had already experienced, and under whose custody he was glad to
place himself. His stay there he found far from
disagreeable, and he spoke with warmth of the
courtesy of the officers in walking out with him
every day, and keeping up their necessary sur-
veillance over his person in a manner that made it
not at all unpleasant. The grand jury soon after
found a bill against him for " the crime of kidnapping an American citizen, *name unknown;*" and he
was held to bail in the sum of $2000, which was
at once forthcoming from a gentleman on the
Canadian side. The result of the trial was against
the prisoner, but a higher tribunal subsequently
quashed the proceedings of the court, and set the
culprit at liberty.

This relation, the particulars of which I have
since found are familiar to the older residents of
Detroit, seemed, from the unaffected yet animated
manner in which it was made, to strike every one
present; and, as you may imagine, our interest in
the party chiefly concerned was not a little heightened by our discovering the next morning, that the
individual who had made himself so agreeable the
evening before was Captain V—— of the British
Navy, whose enviable reputation, as the companion of Captain Owen in his recent arduous

voyage of discovery along the coast of Africa, gives one the privilege of mentioning his name as that of a public man.   Captain V—— has just settled on a farm on the Canada side, but so near to Detroit that his society will be an acquisition to a neighbourhood remarkable for its agreeableness and elegant hospitality.

I have made several excursions to different places in the vicinity of Detroit.   The pleasantest ride, perhaps, is one along the river on the Canada side; from which Detroit appears to great advantage.   Every thing looks dead, however, in William IV.'s dominions, after coming from the bustling American town.   The French there insist upon holding on to their acres, and being unwilling to improve their property, its value remains stationary.   These French tenures have had their effect, too, in retarding the growth of Detroit, and they still check in no slight degree its advances in prosperity.   The French farms are laid out along the river on both sides, with a front of only two or three acres on its bank, while they extend back into the country for half a dozen miles; a disposition of property very unfavourable to agriculture, and only adopted originally to bring the colonists as near together as possible, for the sake of mutual protection against the Indians.   Many of these farms now cross the main street of Detroit at right angles at the upper end of the town, and, of course, offer on either side a dozen building lots of great value. The original owners, however, persist in occupying them with their frail wooden tenements and almost valueless improvements, notwithstanding large sums are continually offered for the merest slice in the world off the end of their long-tailed patrimonies. They are a singular race of beings altogether. Mild and amiable, with all that politeness of manner which distinguishes every class of the courteous nation from which they derived their origin—they are still said to be profoundly ignorant. They call Detroit "the Fort" to this day, and yet few of them know any thing of the country whose soldiers first held it. They are good gardeners, but very indifferent farmers ; and their highest ambition is to turn out the fastest trotting pony when the carriole races commence on the ice at mid-winter. Some of them will own a hundred of these ponies, which, in defiance of snow and sun, run in the woods from one end of the year to the other. The fastest of the herd, which is generally a three-minute horse, the owner will keep for himself, or, if he parts with him, asks the purchaser two or three hundred dollars for the animal, while from the rest, for twenty-five or thirty, he may select at pleasure. They are very easy-gaited animals, carrying astonishing weights with ease; but their shoulders are so low it is difficult to keep an ordinary saddle on their backs with any comfort. But though generally rough mis-shapen looking creatures, some are very elegantly formed, and remind me often—while neither resembling the Arabian nor the English horse—of some French drawings I have seen of the spirited steeds of the Balkan, or the rushing coursers of the Ukraine. I am informed that they are known to perform journeys under the saddle of sixty miles a day for ten days in succession, without being at all injured by it. They are thought to have a different origin from the Canadian horse, to which the best of them bears no particular resemblance except in size.

With judicious crossing, a most valuable race of horses might be produced from this hardy stock, which, for their vigour and endurance, I can only compare to the tough wild thorn of the country; an unpromising shrub, which, when grafted upon, produces the most flourishing fruit-trees I have ever seen.

The drive to Lake St. Clair must be very pleasant in summer, judging from what I saw of it during a raw snowy day. The banks of this river are indeed rather low for beauty, and the lake itself, when you arrive at it, is only a large black sheet of clear water; but the thick-set orchards of the French farmers, coming quite down to the shore of the river, are pleasing objects in themselves, and with the green islands in the strait, the decaying windmills so frequently recurring along its shores, and the groups of shaggy ponies almost invariably grouped around their base, would enable a painter to eke out a very pretty landscape.

About ten miles from Detroit, a United States arsenal is now erecting, under the superintendence of Lieutenant Howard, of the army; for an introduction to whom I was indebted to two young officers, who rode out with me to visit the place. The day was cold and cloudy, like most it has been my lot to describe to you of late; but my companions were intelligent and agreeable, my horse free and sufficiently fast, and my reception at the end so satisfactory, that I still think of my ride along the lazy banks of the bilious-looking River Rouge with pleasure. The arsenal, though of brick, is by far the best specimen of masonry I have yet seen here. It is to be regretted, however, that for such a national work, the appropriation by government for its erection had not been

large enough to have permitted the beautiful
Cleaveland stone, which form the lintels of its
doors and windows, to be substituted for the per-
ishable-looking material of which the building is
now constructed. The taste of Lieutenant H.,
which is already evinced by some arrangements in
the vicinity, will no doubt induce him to preserve
some hoary and fantastic-looking oaks, which fling
their gnarled branches within a few yards of the
walls, and which even now, stripped as they are
of their foliage, are worth a whole forest of common ornamental shrubbery. The trees I have
generally seen around our military posts, look all
as straight and martinet-like as if planted by a
drill-sergeant. These veteran oaks stand upon a
sloping bank, and as they are too crooked ever to
catch the eye of the utilitarian, and be sawed
up into boards, they may, if not now molested,
wave yet for a century above these ingenious
idlers who delight to—

> " ——under the shade of melancholy boughs,
> Lose and neglect the creeping hours of time."

Too much praise can hardly be accorded to the
activity of the officer, who, in five months, has
reared such a building, and created the village
which is already growing up around it in the midst

of an unbroken forest. There is a capital inn, a store, and two or three dwellings in the new town of " Dearbornville," all built since last July. I sat down to dine on a fine haunch of venison, with the veteran General B—— and his young aid, who were together on a hunting expedition in the vicinity. Nothing could have impressed a stranger more favourably with military breeding, than the bland, paternal manner of the gentleman-like old officer to his four juniors present. The deer yet abound within a morning's walk of Detroit ; the primitive forest standing untouched within a few hundred yards of the town, immediately in its rear. They are hunted daily at this season, and no slight sensation was made here a day or two since, by the prolonged absence of the general, who had been benighted and lost his way, upon one of these short excursions. The town was about to turn out en masse, when the reappearance of the hunter, after two days' absence, relieved a very general anxiety.

The tedious length of this letter is sufficient apology for the abruptness with which I must break off.

L 2

LETTER XI.

Monroe, Michigan, Dec. 3, 1833

The drive from Detroit hither is dull enough at this season of the year. The road leads through almost a dead level, and the muddy streams creep over the fat black soil, as if they had gormandized upon its rich vegetation till grown too lazy for locomotion. Among others, the Huron River, from which—seeing that it rises in one of the brightest and most beautiful lakes in the peninsula, better things might be expected, waddles on to the lake, as little excited by the flocks of ducks which frolic on its bosom, as an alderman after dinner by the flies that disport upon his jerkin. Occasionally, indeed, some bright little rill will ripple across the road, and smirk over its yellow pebbles on its way to the big lake, with much the same air that the mill-streams of Long Island dance over the level ground while hurrying to the sea. But a wet prairie soon intervenes, and the innocent rivulet, like a child that is snubbed, becomes at once silent and sulky. But though some parts of Wayne county are thus unattractive, I am told that other sections contain much arable land of excellent quality, consisting of sand loam and some clay with heavy timber, and occasionally fine bottoms along the streams. The population is about eight thousand.

The village of Monroe, in the county of the same name, from which I now write, is situated on the banks of the River Raisin, and about two miles from its entrance into Lake Erie. It was incorporated two years since, and comprises a part of the old site of Frenchtown, celebrated, as you remember, in the annals of the last war. The place is said to be regularly laid out ; but the most business part of it—and it is the fussiest little town in the world—looks as if the buildings had all been tossed from the other side of the river, and left to settle just where they might fall upon this. If the place continues to increase as rapidly, however, as it has during the last year—the population having doubled in that time—the inhabitants can afford to burn down the river side of the village, and arrange it to more advantage. There are now about 150 houses, of which 20 or 30 are stone ; some of them are wholesale establishments, and make a very handsome display of fancy goods. There are also two grist-mills immediately in the town, a woollen factory, an iron foundry, several saw-mills, a chair factory, a tannery, &c. And yet, notwithstanding the supply of water-power affords every facility for the use of machinery, the demand for manual labour is very great, and mechanics of every kind may here, as in Detroit, find constant employment. Indeed, I am told, that the demand for mechanics in every part of Michigan is excessive; and as for labourers, I have seen them repeatedly advertised for, by written notices on tavern doors and elsewhere. The emigrants to the territory, I find, are generally people of a very respectable class, who have both the disposition and the means to employ the services of others around them.

The "Bank of the River Raisin" is established at this place, with a capital of $100,000; and though in its infancy, is said to be doing a very flourishing business. The notes are among the handsomest specimens of bank-note engraving I have seen. There is also a Land-Office established here, at which the sales of public lands since last April amount to upwards of $22,000; the sales at Detroit and White Pigeon together a little exceeding this sum. The government price of land ($100 for 80 acres) being the same in every part of the territory, this will give you some idea of the immigration into the Peninsula.

I must not forget to mention that with a population of only 1600 souls, five religious denominations are represented in their respective clergymen at Monroe; and that three of these, the Roman Catholic, Episcopal, and Presbyterian, have each a neat church of their own. I ought to add that a newspaper, with a good circulation, is printed here.

The advantageous position of Monroe, situated as it is at the head of Lake Erie, induced the government to make an appropriation for improving the harbour, which, except that of Maumee, is the only one at this part of the lake. The lamented Major Maurice, of the Engineer Corps (who, you may remember, fell down and instantly expired in the act of shaking hands with General Gratiot at Washington, last winter), and whom the inhabitants of this place speak of with the tenderest remembrance—made minute surveys of the harbour and of the different channels of the river; and the bill which has been at various times introduced into Congress for their improvement was based upon his reports. A bill was passed at the last session of Congress appropriating $8,000 for rebuilding the pier at the mouth of the river, and also appropriating the sum of $20,000 for a road from La Plaisance bay, through which the Raisin debouches into Lake Erie, to intersect the Chicago road, which traverses the whole Peninsula at a point about 40 miles from here; an improvement which will open a new market to southern and western Michigan, and contribute of course much to the prosperity of Monroe. A bill was also passed by both houses appropriating $15,000 for a canal connecting the waters of Lake Erie and the River Raisin, by a cut across the bar at the mouth of the latter. The money has not been expended, however, in consequence of an oversight in the engrossing clerk, which, from his omitting this important item, has prevented the bill as yet becoming a law. The moneys appropriated for the pier and road have already been mostly expended, and those public works are now nearly completed under the active and efficient superintendence of Capt. Henry Smith, of the Engineer Corps. When all these improvements are completed, Monroe must come in for a large share of the immense trade and commerce which must flow through the three outlets of eastern Michigan. The mouth of the Maumee can hardly compete with it on account of the extreme unhealthiness of that swampy region; but I am inclined to think that the enterprising inhabitants of this thriving little place are somewhat too vivacious in their expectations, when they think of not only rivalling, but outstripping, the ancient city of the straits on the onward road to prosperity. Detroit, like every other point selected by the French on the Western waters of our country, is as commanding a position, whether for war or trade, as could be chosen.

The Monroeites are, however, a driving people in their way. They are now building a steamboat of the largest class, which will cost not less than $45,000, to ply directly between here and Buffalo; and this morning I saw launched a beautiful schooner, for the lake navigation. It was the first launch that had ever taken place at Monroe, and the occasion caused a general turn out of the inhabitants, who hurried to the spot, a mile or two off, upon horses of every variety of appearance. There was the bull-necked French pony and his scraggy looking Indian cousin, the sleek spongy-looking Ohio horse, and the clean-limbed quickly-gathering Kentuckian, galloping between the swift but shuffling Illinois pacer, and the high-actioned tight-looking New-York trotter. Every one rode as if for a wager, and when we drew our reins the talk upon horse flesh superseding almost the interest of the schooner, showed that the Monroe-ites, like Catiline and Purdy, deserve to be cele-

brated for their judgment in these matters. A
very good and full band of Amateur Musicians,
composed of respectable private individuals of the
village, came at last upon the ground, and changed
the subject to the name of the new vessel, which
several wished to alter before launching, from the
hackneyed one of Diana to the more characteristic
sound of *Tecumseh*, the spot being so celebrated in
the memoirs of that great chief. "You knew Tecumseh then, sir?" said I to an old gentleman, who,
I was informed, had been a field officer during the
late war, and engaged in several battles. "I did,
sir, and he was as thorough a gentleman and as high-
toned an officer as any in the British service."
The chief, you know, actually held his commission
as a general officer immediately from the King of
Britain. "What do you then, sir, think of his massacre upon this spot," I rejoined. "The *barbarity*
of that act, sir, was only in accordance with Indian
ideas of warfare. The *disgrace* of it attaches entirely to the English officer (Proctor) who permitted,
perhaps sanctioned, the atrocity." The old officer's
blood seemed to kindle anew as he dwelt upon that
horrible slaughter of a force which had capitulated
on honourable terms with a full reliance on the foe
for protection. I asked him about the sick and
wounded, who were burnt up in the hospital, or

shot to death as they ran shrieking through the flames. "I saw their bones," he replied, "when the ruins were still recent. I came on with the corps of Kentuckians which advanced soon after into this country, and subsequently so eagerly avenged their countrymen at the battle of the Thames.* I walked to the spot where the wounded met their fate, with several others. Richard M. Johnson was one of the number. We looked into the pit, and could see the charred bones and dismembered limbs, and sometimes half-burnt bodies, plainly below. The men muttered the deepest curses. Col. J. spoke not a word, but the tears rained from his eyes; and turning away, he exclaimed, 'There lies the best blood in Kentucky, poured out like water.'" I have given as nearly as I can the very words of the veteran colonel in describing this sad spectacle. Of the seven hundred young men murdered here, the most were students at law, young physicians, and merchants, and the sons of opulent farmers,—in short, the very flower of Kentucky.† The event threw the whole State into mourning.

* See note C.

† Since this.was written, I have met with a Kentucky gentleman in Illinois, who had lost five relations in the massacre—a father, two brothers, an uncle, and a cousin—the youngest was not seventeen.

Speaking of the troops who were concerned in the early operations of these regions, I have heard a number of interesting accounts from different persons of the formation of the several corps. One of these, though I may very probably, in trying to recall the particulars, confound them with the incidents of another, I will venture to repeat. A graduate of Williams College, Massachusetts, who had been recently admitted to the bar, was riding through the State of Kentucky, perhaps with the design of finding some favourable point at which to fix his abode and commence the practice of his profession, when he was accosted near a village by a mounted traveller, who, mentioning that he was a planter of the country, invited the young advocate, with all the freedom of western hospitality, to dine at his house the following day. The invitation was accepted ; and the eastern gentleman, arriving at the mansion of the unknown host, found a large party collected, the majority of whom were well acquainted with each other, while many were strangers like himself, and invited apparently in the same manner. The dinner, however, was got through with sociably enough ; and by the time the glass began to circulate freely, all felt that easy confidence in the fellowship and good feeling of each other which is the soul of good society. The host, then rising, described briefly the state of the north-western frontier, and produced a commission from his pocket to raise a corps and march at once thither. They enlisted to a man; their entertainer provided them on the spot with the necessary stores and munitions; and the band of volunteers started in a few hours on their march to the border.

The name of the noble host was not mentioned, but the eastern adventurer, who was elected a lieutenant upon the spot, and soon after became a captain, was said to have been better known since as colonel, general, governor, and lastly,—Mr. Secretary Cass.

I regret now that I did not inquire into and note down the names and other particulars of a relation so striking, but you have the tale as it was told in my hearing, *minus* the admirable manner of the relation. But I am forgetting the Diana—that burst of music tells that she begins to move on her ways--calmly now she slides like a pair of Broqua's slippers through a quadrille; and now, as that bottle of champaign foams over her bow, her motion increases almost to the velocity of a *gallope*. What a sensation does she make among the waves, and how do they coquet with her on every side! She bobs about till she seems as unstable as themselves. But now the sober skipper, like a good husband, takes possession of her virgin charms, and placing himself at once at the helm, the unmeaning waters cease their flirting, and sustain her above them without daring to attempt to influence her course.

The ride to these dock-yards is rather pleasant; but I have seen handsomer rivers than the Raisin. The banks for several miles around the village have been almost denuded of trees; and the limestone channel lets off so much of the stream through its crevices, that, like a tankard of liquor passed round, according to custom, at a western inn, it is half drunk up before it gets to its real owner, the lake. It would delight an eastern farmer, to see the magnificent pear-trees which, tall as the trees of the forest, and of the growth of a century, extend through orchards for miles along the stream. Here, too, are apple-trees, to the excellence of whose fruit I can testify, that were brought by the French to this country in 1731. The grape-vines, also, from which the river takes its name, constitute a beautiful feature in the level landscape, as they hang in rich festoons along the banks of the stream, and climb wherever it is wooded to the tops of the loftiest elms.

There is now an application and great interest

making to incorporate a company for the purpose of improving the navigation of the River Raisin and the Saline by a lock and dam navigation,—an improvement which it is said can be made at slight expense. The river, flowing gently in its channel, with banks of equal elevation, seems ready to receive and bear upon its bosom the rich products of the country on its borders. By constructing a tow-path, the expense of which will not be heavy, an excellent canal can be easily made.

The subject of canals and railroads awakens at this moment the keenest interest in Michigan ; and, after the route of the projected grand communication between Lakes Erie and Michigan, through the peninsula, shall be determined upon by the general government, I have no doubt but that large and advantageous outlays of private capital upon similar works will be made at other points. Of the plans talked of as best worthy the attention of government, that of a grand railroad from Chicago to Detroit, with a lateral one perhaps to Monroe, seems to be considered as the least chimerical ; though there are not a few who advocate a canal immediately across the peninsula, in a direct line from the mouth of the Maumee to Lake Michigan ; and still a greater number who urge the construction of one from the mouth of the Raisin to that of the St. Joseph's, on the opposite side of the peninsula—a route which would pass through a country acknowledged, I believe, to be the most fertile in Michigan. But another project still remains, as feasible, or perhaps more so than either of these. It is to connect the Washtenong or Grand River— a noble stream, which waters half the territory, and is navigable nearly 240 miles in bateaux—with the Huron, a fine stream, which, after rising within a few miles of the sources of the Washtenong, empties into Lake Erie, on the opposite side of the peninsula. You can hardly form an idea of the relative importance and feasibility of these projects, without more knowledge of the territory of Michigan than is common at the east, where people generally know about as much of it as they do of Timbuctoo. I have already been so fortunate in my opportunities of talking with well-informed people here, that I might venture at once to give you a general view of the country, but I prefer that you should gather whatever information I have to give from my own actual observations made along the road. With regard to scenery, I do not think, from what I have yet seen, I can promise you much; but for agricultural and mineral resources, and for manufacturing and commercial advantages, I think I can produce some data which, if they do not astonish our good people at home in regard to Michigan, will at least account for the emigrants pouring into the territory as they do, and believing it to be the garden of the Union. You must, however, pick up your information as I shall, by jogging along quietly with me through the country, and observing matters and things just as they come beneath our eyes. To-morrow I start for the interior. Farewell.

LETTER XII.

Monroe Co., M. T., Dec. 5, 1833.

I write to you from a log-cabin on the banks of the river Raisin, about thirty miles above Monroe. The worthy farmer, upon whose premises I am quartered for the night, sits with his child on his knee, in the chimney-corner, with a prosing visiter, pipe in mouth, opposite, while the good woman is engaged doing some " chores" at the farther end of the apartment, which is, of course, the chief cooking, eating, sitting, sleeping, and smoking chamber in the house. My dormitory, I have a shrewd suspicion, is to be in a loft, from which a lad is at this moment descending by a ladder with some corn for my horse. The black walnut stand, upon which I am writing, occupies the centre of the room ; and as I am at this moment keeping up my share in a desultory conversation going forward around me, and at the same time trying to check the undue familiarity of a large bull-dog— who, like other individuals, has become troublesome from being admitted too rapidly into intimacy

—you must not expect me to be very coherent in detailing the impressions of the day.

It was a gloomy, lowering morning, with occasional flakes of snow driving through the harsh atmosphere, when I started from the village of Monroe, well mounted on a stout roan, whose figure and action would command thrice the sum in New-York that the animal cost me here, and whose performance to-day speaks well of the dependence I may place upon him to carry me through my arduous route into the interior of the Peninsula. It was with a feeling of almost boyish pleasure that, after the slight taste I have had of stage-coach travelling from Pittsburg to Cleveland, and from Detroit to Monroe, I found myself once more in the saddle, with the full privilege of regulating my motions as I choose. The delightful mode in which I travelled with S—— from New-York to Wheeling, in a barouche, with two led horses under the saddle, was, indeed, both for pleasure and solid comfort, not to be surpassed. But now, though I have neither the agreeable friend, the attentive groom, nor the luxurious carriage to enhance the gratification and relieve the weariness of travelling, the feeling of independence still remains. And though I confess I could not suppress a sigh this morning, when packing up the linen and books which, with my trunk, I shall not see for a month to come ; yet that pair of saddle-bags beneath my feet, though conscious only of a shirt apiece, flanked as they are by my light fowling-piece, which that weather-beaten worthy is at this moment curiously examining, and my leggings, which are drying upon those andirons, make me feel as rich as did that famous soldato Dugald Dalgetty himself, with his single change of chamois leather and iron overcoat, while handling his arms and surveying his compact appointments from the back of the doughty Gustavus.

My road led, from the moment of leaving the village, along the banks of the Raisin, whose serpentine current flowed fuller and clearer the farther I advanced into the country. The land at the same time gradually rising, and though never hilly, yet leaving the stream far enough below to form a bluff of some ten or fifteen feet, where the timber-land rose from the rich bottoms on its margin. After riding thus for about twenty miles along the river, where the log-cabins gradually became fewer and farther between, I struck through a wood so dense that it seemed to terminate the settlements in this direction, and then at a sudden turning of the path, I came at once upon the " oak openings." It would be difficult to convey an idea of the pleasing effect of such a surprise. Imagine yourself emerging from a New-Jersey swamp, and coming at one bound upon one of the English parks which Puckler Muskaw so admirably describes. Clumps of the noblest oaks, with not a twig of underwood, extending over a gently undulating grassy surface as far as the eye can reach; here clustered together in a grove of tall stems supporting one broad canopy of interlacing branches, and there rearing their gigantic trunks in solitary grandeur from the plain. The feeling of solitude I had while in the deep woods deserted me the moment I came upon this beautiful scene, and I rode on for hours, unable without an effort to divest myself of the idea that I was in a cultivated country.

Towards evening I found myself in the thick forest again, and was glad, as the night closed in darkly over the road where at every step my horse would either sink to his knees in mud, or trip over the stubble of newly cut saplings, to be overtaken by a mail-rider, with his leathern charge on horseback. The lonely lad was as glad of company through the forest as I was of a guide; and he willingly taking the lead, I flung my bridle on my horse's neck, as the skies became blacker and blacker, and touching him smartly with the spur, away we went through the woods together.—

" Take care of that tree, sir; look out for the mud-hole"—called my goblin usher at each moment, as we tramped and splashed along, where I would have defied the Evil One himself to have seen any thing but the impenetrable dark. I heeded him not; but bending low in the saddle to avoid the boughs, and gluing my knees to the surcingle, I surrendered myself to my destiny, and attended to nothing but keeping my horse as close as possible to the heels of his file leader. At length we reached a clearing, and a few yards of better road brought us to a log-cabin. The family were at supper when I entered; and sitting down with the rest, I helped myself with an iron spoon from a dish of suppawn, and fishing up a cup from the bottom of a huge pan of milk, I poured the snowy liquid over the boiled meal that rivalled it in whiteness. The corn, from which it is made, my host tells me, grew to the height of sixteen feet, the stalks being of a blackish green colour. From the same soil, a black sandy loam of easy tillage, wheat as high as a man's head has been raised; the produce from a single grain being from 300 to 400, and in one instance one thousand and twenty-six. I see symptoms of sleeping in those around me; and having no right to monopolize this important apartment, will conclude this elsewhere to-morrow.

Tecumseh, Lenawee Co., M. T., Dec. 6.

The cockloft, as I expected, was my place of rest. I stumbled over a pile of corn, and struck my head against the roof, almost as soon as I had got my body fairly above the trap-door. I found a clean bed, however, and it was a very sociable place after all; for there were four persons besides myself stowed away in the different corners. So soundly did I sleep on my straw pallet, that the night seemed to me but just begun, when the red glare of a tallow candle flashing over my eyes, with the tap of the mail rider on my shoulder, told me that dawn was breaking, and that we must be gone. The landlord brought out a lantern for me to. mount by; and we had proceeded far on our journey before the faintest streak in the East indicated the waking of the sun.

It was about seven o'clock, when, stopping to water at a little shantee, I found several labouring people at breakfast within; and the mail carrier consenting to wait for me, I sat down at table at once with the rest. The fare consisted of hot rolls and tea, with large pieces of pork swimming in its gravy, with a plate of noble potatoes, that pulverized when you touched them. My plate was heaped at once with all, while each one present vied with the other in civility to me. They were talking of a horse, for which a hundred dollars had been paid, when I entered; and an English poaching gun I have with me, not worth a fifth of the sum, caught the fancy of the owner. He insisted upon " swapping with me on equal terms," and seemed much hurt when I refused not only to " trade," but expressed no inclination to see his favourite steed. I replied, however, so good humouredly to his entreaties, that he still persisted in them until taken aside by one or two of those present. He then came up to me in an altered manner—" I hope, sir, that I don't insult you by wanting to buy that *curiosest* of guns, for I don't mean to be uncivil—not at all—in the least." Upon assuring him that I had taken no offence, he rejoined, that if his horse was not worth two hundred dollars he would eat him, but he had set his heart upon that gun, and must have it. I did not like to expose myself to the temptation of seeing the horse, though of course I did not think for a moment of taking advantage of the honest yeoman's caprice; but had it not been a present from a friend abroad, I should certainly have given my ardent acquaintance the toy which caught his fancy after what followed. " I say, stranger," said he, musing for a moment, " do you want a farm, eh! a house, eh! I'll trade you as good a tavern stand, two miles from this, as there is in the county." I got away at last as he followed me to the door, and held my bridle to mount, by promising to leave him the object of his desires in my will.

The character of the country continued for some miles much the same as that passed over yesterday, though the river gradually degenerated into a narrow, muddy stream. The log-cabins which always occurred in the heavily-timbered district, had nothing to distinguish them from each other, and the openings were as silent as if man and beast had deserted them ; though I saw a couple of deer in one instance feeding afar off, and met a settler who was carrying a wolf, just caught in a trap by the road-side, on his shoulders. I was struck, too, at seeing no less than three pet fawns near different houses, within a few miles of each other. In one instance a tall hound was sitting erect beside one of these gentle creatures, who was licking the ears of the enemy of his race. The incident reminded me of an anecdote I heard told by an old hunter in one of the wild mountain districts of New-York. His favourite hound, one morning, when the deer were in the red coat and not fit to hunt, came to him while chopping, and made signs for his master to follow to a thicket not far off, where the woodman discovered a fawn so entangled that it could not escape. It was so small and feeble that he carried it away with ease in his arms, while the doe, which was near at hand, followed her bleating offspring. The dog accompanied him with great apparent joy, and, though one of the keenest of his kind, would drive off the grown deer only a few rods, and then return at once to keep an eye on his master's movements. The fawn was taken home, and, being fed continually by the children, soon went tame about the house. The dog, however, insisted upon sleeping with it, and could scarcely be separated from his long-eared friend; and when it met with the usual fate of pets, and died prematurely, a month or two after, poor Ring was inconsolable. The worthy English settler, who had been a gamekeeper in the "*auld* country" in his day, added, that he had the curiosity to dress a piece of the venison, which, fond as hounds are of that food, was rejected with disgust by the canine mourner.

One of the other fawns which I saw, would, with the group attendant, have made a pretty subject for Fisher's pencil. He had thrust his head into a bevy of rosy little girls, who were making "sand pies" on the bank of the river; and as his delicate hoofs threatened to demolish the rural substitutes for the card-houses of parlour-bred urchins, one of the little architects, covering her work with her hands, kept the intrusive animal at bay with her head ; the long yellow locks of which streamed over his bluish crest, while the perverse beast twisted his snout under and insisted upon licking her face.

It was still early in the afternoon when I arrived at this place, and my surprise was not slight, after coming through a region where every mile seemed to lead me farther from civilization, to light suddenly upon a pretty village laid out with broad streets, and having an excellent tavern on a public square in the centre. I entered the town through an oak opening. Within a few hundred yards from the village I passed a half-dozen graves, apparently dug at random among the trees, though each was ornamented with a handsome head-stone. I have since learned that the town's people, with a degree of consideration which might well be emulated in larger cities, are already making arrangements to lay out and plant a public cemetery for the use of every religious denomination in the place. At Monroe, I believe they have already done the same thing. There, indeed, they had an ample number of guests for the narrow house, before even the abodes for the living were built. The bones of those massacred on the Raisin, bleached till within a few years on the banks of that river; and an inhabitant of the place told me that he had often walked over the execution-ground and handled sculls that were cloven with the tomahawk. There is also an Indian cemetery about twelve miles from Monroe, where the skeletons of the dead can be plainly seen through the crevices of the stone-pile heaped above them. I am told that they are wholly unmolested by the white inhabitants; partly from feelings of decency creditable to themselves, and partly, perhaps, from fear of the roving relatives of the deceased, who return yearly and observe the condition of the spot with a jealous eye. Not far from this place resides an old settler, who has killed a half a dozen Indians with his own hand. Three or four of them he shot with his rifle from his cabin, when they surrounded it to capture him; and the stories told of his encounters with the others might better be detailed by a novelist than a letter-writer. I have seen nothing of the natives yet, except a couple of Wyandott squaws; though the French settlers, with their elf locks and blanket capotes, might at a distance be well taken for aborigines. I think a little of starting at once for the rapids of the Grand River, and spending a week or two among the Ottowas, who, I am told, are still there in considerable numbers, and preserving enough of their original habits to make them fair specimens of the Michigan Indians. They tell me, however, that a guide will be indispensable ; and having already offered one in vain a fair compensation, I may be compelled to give up the attempt.

The Grand River, or Washtenong, is, as I have before mentioned, the largest stream in the Peninsula, being 270 miles in length, while the country watered by it consists of about 7,000 square miles. It has a good harbour at its mouth, on Lake Michigan, for vessels drawing eight feet water, and it is navigable for those drawing four feet for more than thirty miles from the lake : while farther inland it traverses a country represented by my informant, who has recently returned from surveying in that distant region, as of immense fertility. There are also beds of gypsum and lime, with stone-quarries and mines of iron, with indications of the existence of copper, to be found on its tributaries, while a hundred mineral springs—which seem to abound in this country, for I have already seen a half a dozen—enrich the central region where its branches interlock with the bright waters of the Huron on the eastern, and the myriads of streams and lakes which form the sources of the Kekalamazoo, on the western side of the Peninsula.

They tell me here that it would be in vain for me to attempt to cross the country from Chicago to St. Louis alone at this season of the year, when, if the vast prairies are covered with snow, I should be lost beyond a certainty; and as I am now compelled to remain until the new public conveyance, contracted for by government, commences running on the first of January, I shall employ the intermediate time in seeing as much of Michigan as possible. I find myself among the most intelligent population of the middle class (the bone and sinew of a community) I ever mixed with; and every one seems so contented, may even say delighted, with his adopted home, that I am catching a little of the spirit of those around me, and am eager to visit more intimately scenes, which one would suppose were Elysian, by the way in which people talk of them. I find myself as yet only thirty-five miles from Monroe by the new U. S. road, though the route I travelled was sixty-five. When you next hear from me I shall be farther in the interior, and hope to be able to tell you that I have seen a hill or a rock, the sight of either of which would, I confess, be refreshing, in spite of all the charms of oak openings, vine-hung streams, and grassy bottoms.

LETTER XIII.

Saline, Washtenaw Co., M. T., Dec. 7.

I have just spent an hour with Mr. Risden, the surveyor of a great part of Michigan, at whose house I have stopped for the night, in talking about the district with which he is familiar ; and I shall avail myself of the information thus acquired, in filling up hereafter my notes upon the country. The conversation turning upon the healthfulness of Michigan, there was not one out of several residents present who did not allow the existence of bilious fevers and fever and ague, in every part of the country ; but they spoke of passing through these diseases as merely a slight process of *acclimating*, which, in the general health of the country, was hardly to be considered. They asserted, too, what I have before heard stated by more than one physician in the territory, that Michigan is exempt from many of the diseases most fatal to human life at the East. Consumption, for instance,—which a reference to the bills of mortality will show destroys almost as many in New-York, take year and year together for several in succession,* as does the yellow-fever in New-Orleans,—is here unknown.   Not only, I am told, do no cases originate here, but many persons from New-York, it is pretended, have been cured of the complaint by coming to reside in Michigan.   The most un-healthy points are in the vicinity of mill-dams, and of marshes, near both of which the settlers take particular pains to "locate ;" the first for the convenience of grinding and sawing, and near the last for the rich grass they afford with only the trouble of mowing.   Health, indeed, is the last thing a settler seems to think of, by the way in which he chooses a site for his house.   In a coun-try so abounding with lakes and streams of the purest water, and filled with fish, that you may pass a dozen in a ride of as many miles, you but seldom find a house on their banks ; while the pur-chaser of a new possession neglects alike the tempting-looking oak·opening, and erects his dwell-ing in the thick forest, provided only a road or trail passes within three feet of his door.   A trail, by-the-way, I must tell you, is an Indian footpath,

* Unless I am much mistaken, the deaths from consumption alone average twenty-five a week, which will give 12 or 1400 fatal cases in a year; a terrible result from one complaint alone.

that has been travelled perhaps for centuries, and bears here the same relation to an ordinary road that a turnpike does to a railroad in your state. He chooses, in short, the most fertile spot on his acres, in order to have a garden immediately around his house, which he places plump upon the road, in order to have it " more sociable-like, and see folks passing." His garden grows from almost nothing. The first year the hog-pen and cow-yard occupy the place designed for its commencement. They are moved farther from the house the second year, and a few cabbages occupy the place which they have enriched by their temporary situation upon it. They move again on the third year ; and the garden, which can now boast of a few currant-bushes and a peach-tree, expands over the place they have ceased to occupy. And now our settler, having built a fine barn, and " got things snug about him," begins to like the looks of the woods again, which he has so industriously swept from every spot that can be seen from his door. He shoulders his pickaxe, goes out into the forest, and selecting two of the straightest maple saplings he can find, they are at once disinterred, their heads chopped off, to make these tall awkward things look civilized, and the pair of poles, thrust into the ground within two feet of his door, are whitewashed and called trees.

Dexter, Washtenaw Co., M. T., Dec. 12.

I have been here two or three days; but so occupied in riding about looking at the country, that I have not till now attempted to finish this letter. Far different is the appearance of the cottages here from those described above, as the common residence of new settlers. They build almost altogether in the oak openings; and as the country is now undulating, I have seen some cabins very prettily situated in clumps of oaks, a gun-shot from the road, with fields of young wheat extending in every direction around them. The soil, when first turned up, is a kind of yellow gravel, very unpromising in its appearance; but it rapidly undergoes a chymical change, becoming almost black in fields of two years' cultivation, and improving every season without the aid of a particle of manure. I have now got among the rolling land, in a region full of lakes and oak openings, of which hitherto I had only a taste. I need hardly say how much more grateful such a country is to my eye than the level thickly-timbered lands about Detroit and Monroe.

I came hither by way of the pretty village of

Anne-Arbour, which contains, I should think, seven or eight hundred inhabitants; many of whom, I am told, are very respectable English emigrants. I stopped at a farm-house, about five miles from here, to dine. A white-headed boy, six or seven years old, was turning a grindstone before the door, while a couple of Indians sharpened their knives. Near them a miserable pony, with his wooden saddle covered with a freshly-flayed deer, and a brindled, wiry-haired dog, with the head of a wolf and the crest of a boar, skulked around the slaughtered game, and snarled in its protection, when, after dismounting, I approached it. His swarthy masters and myself entered the house together. " *Tenepe keen chemocomon?*" (Where is your American?) said the oldest of the two to a very pretty Connecticut girl, who had recently followed her husband to this country. She, replied by pointing to him, working at a distance in a field, and the Indians sat down patiently till the farmer entered. The venison was then laid on a table, and a bargaining scene commenced, which lasted full half an hour. " *Cau-nee-shin, chomocomon*" (Not a good American), said one of the red barterers, turning to me, as the white trader offered him what he thought too little for a whole deer. The bargain was struck, however

before a by-stander could interpret the appeal for
me. The skin still remained with the Indian, and
I was not a little surprised to see produced from
it a variety of articles of Indian produce, among
which were large cakes of deer's tallow, about
the size of an ordinary cheese. These were all
traded away in succession, and a small cask produced by the Indian was filled with whiskey on
the spot; and the eldest mounting the pony, they
both shook me by the hand, and soon disappeared
with their poisonous burden behind a turning of
the road. They were of the Ottawa tribe, well-
made men, though slightly built, and with aquiline
noses and finely-shaped heads; and each, when I
first saw them, had the freest and most graceful step
I ever saw, whether on the sod or in the ball-room.
How complete was the metamorphosis when I
overtook them half an hour afterward in the
woods! The eldest, who could not have been
more than five-and-thirty, was barely sober enough
to guide his horse, and sitting with both arms
around the barrel of whiskey on the pommel
before him, he reminded me of an engraving of
Bacchus, in a very vulgar and not very witty
book, called Homer Travestie. The Indian gravity, which had before been preserved amid all the
nervousness incident to a trading operation, had

now thoroughly deserted him, and toddling from side to side, he muttered a sort of recitative, which combined all the excellences of the singing and spouting of a civilized toper. His companion, a youth of but seventeen, seemed perfectly sober, and stopping only occasionally to pick up the whip of the fumbling rider, he stepped so lightly by his horse's side that the leaves scarcely rustled beneath his moccasin. I was somewhat pained, of course, at the exhibition, though I confess I was not a little diverted, while riding along for miles in the silent woods, with such grotesque company. The pedestrian continued as reserved and respectful as ever; but my fellow-cavalier, after talking a quantity of gibberish to me, which was, of course, perfectly unintelligible, seemed to be at last quite angry because I could not understand him; then, after again becoming pacified, he found a new source of vehemence in urging me to " *schwap pasischegun*" (exchange my gun, to which he took a great fancy) for his " *papooshe pascocachee*" (child of a horse), as he called a colt that followed the forlorn pony on which he rode. I could not help blaming myself, however, for having been so long diverted with the frailties of this hospitable Silenus, when at parting, about nightfall, where he struck into the forest, he gave me an invitation to his wigwam, twenty miles off, signifying the distance by raising all his fingers twice, at the same time using the words, "*Howh! keen marchee neen wigwam*" (come to my wigwam). How strangely are we constituted, that one should derive amusement in the woods from an exhibition which, in a city, would only excite pain and disgust! I have never seen a half-intoxicated Indian before without the deepest feelings of commiseration. As for the alleged crime of selling Indians whiskey, it is impossible to prevent it. The love of spirituous liquors is a natural craving of the red man, which is irrepressible, and as such I have heard the most humane and intelligent persons speak of it,—people who have passed their lives among the Indians, and have done their best to snatch them from this perdition. The haughtiest chief will travel a hundred miles for a pint of whiskey, and get drunk the moment he receives it, wheresoever he may be. Providence seems to have designed that this mysterious race should not continue upon the earth, and fate has infused a fatal thirst into their bosoms, which is hastening their doom with fearful celerity. But six years ago, and the woods around me were alive with Indians; now they are only traversed by a few such stragglers as these. You may talk of civilizing them,—but that, too, is impossible.

You may more easily civilize the stupidest African than the most intelligent Indian ; and yet, who for a moment would compare the erect port and manly tread, the air, the *blooded* look of the one, with his keen sagacity and rare instincts, to the misshapen form, the shuffling gait, and stupid bearing of the other ? Where, then, lies the difficulty ? The African is an imitative animal,—the Indian is not. He will copy the form of your weapons, for he has felt their edge ; and he will make himself ridiculous by wearing a cocked hat, because he conceives it to be an emblem of authority. Rings and bracelets he may wear, for they recommend him to his own tribe ; but the forms and fashions of civilization he despises. The negro furnishes the best raw material for a dandy that can be had ; he learns at once how to wear his hat and adjust his shirt-collar, according to the last mode of the white man. The Indian, if a fop, departs even further than usual from the costume of a European. He comes from Nature's hands all that she ever intended him to be,—the wild man of the woods. To the fleetness of the deer in traversing the forest, he unites the instinct of the hound in finding his way ; and when you add to these the mental gift of a certain wild eloquence, wholly unimprovable by cultivation, you have nearly summed up the intellectual qualifications of the American savage,—the genuine child of nature —the untamed—the untameable.

I had a long conversation on this subject yesterday with a middle-aged gentleman of high intelligence and character, for many years settled in the territory, and who has availed himself of unusual opportunities of studying Indian life and manners. We had been all day in a canoe, paddled by ourselves, exploring a chain of small lakes in this vicinity; and the perfect stillness of the woods around, while floating at sunset over the transparent water, induced him to remark upon the rapid disappearance of the inhabitants; who, but six years since, when he first visited this part of Michigan, kept their canoes upon every stream in the country.   The observation suggested the discussion, already alluded to, upon the feasibility of civilizing the Indians; and he told me a variety of anecdotes about a young Ottawa chief with an unpronounceable name, whom, on various accounts, he had once thought the fittest subject for social life he had ever met with among the aborigines. The conclusion of his relation was so whimsical and strikingly characteristic, that I will finish this letter with the details precisely as I took them down in my note-book from the lips of my informant; our canoe, the while, being allowed to float as she listed along the placid bosom of one of those beautiful lakes into which the river Huron expands a few miles from its sources.

"As we came one day to the Indian encampment, Ketche-waun-doug-enink caught me by the hand as usual, with his shrill exclamation of welcome, and my party proceeded at once to pitch our tent near his, before a blazing fire of logs. After affording us what assistance he could, the young chief left us; but in the evening he called in again at our tent, and brought his father and mother, his wife, and three sisters with him. They all looked quite solemn, and in his manner, particularly, there was something altogether unusual. Young Ketche-waun-doug-enink had been quite my friend, always appeared glad to see me, and was generally sociable in his way, but now he was grave and reserved, almost to severity. My familiarity with Indian character induced me to suppress every thing like surprise at such an extraordinary change of deportment, and we sat thus, I should think, for at least half an hour. At last the young Indian rose up in a formal way, and taking a position full in the light of the fire, began a speech abounding with gesture and vehemence. The amount of it was this:—' Listen, my friend; I see that you are wiser than any of your white brethren.'—['I must interrupt my story,' said my companion, 'to remind you, that believing my young Indian friend, who was a fine-looking fellow, had some relish for civilization, and half a mind, indeed, to turn white man, I anticipated that some proposition to that effect would be the purport of his speech.']—He continued—'I am glad to see that you love the Indians; that you are not ashamed of our mode of life. Let me tell you, what I presume you already know, that the life of the white man is one of care and trouble. The Great Spirit has blessed his red children in a peculiar manner. We have no care. We are as Che-manitou* made us. We have not degenerated, but are still his favourites. You never see a wrinkle on the brow of an Indian. Look, my brother, at the forehead of my old father: it is as smooth as my own, though sixty winters have whitened his head. His days have glided on as undisturbed as the smooth stream before you.'—['We were on the banks of the Shiawassee,' interrupted the narrator.]—'Do you see, my brother, those pebbles in the bottom of the clear stream as it throws back the light of your fire? It is thus that every thought can be

---

} * Che-manitou, God, or the Great Spirit; Mi-che-manitou, the devil, or the evil spirit.—See note D.

seen that dwells in the mind of the Indian. He
has no disguise—no cause for it—the troubles of
the white man disturb not the clear stream of his
soul.   Come with us—share with us the gifts of
Che-manitou—think no more of those distant lands
of your childhood, where men live but to harass
each other, and gather riches that eat the soul up
with care—come—here you will build your wigwam—I will help you—you shall have my sister
for your wife—she shall weave your mats, and
raise your corn, and dry your venison, which we
will kill together in the woods.   You have lived
long enough a life of wretchedness; come and be
happy with us.' "

I was curious to learn how the rest of the
family, and especially the fair member of it particularly designated in this singular harangue, be-
haved while her brother was pronouncing it ; and
more than all, how the object of it himself received
the address.   I will endeavour to give you the
exact replies of my interesting companion, without
repeating the various questions from me which
elicited them.

" My young friend sat down.   Throughout his
speech, the family observed the utmost silence.
The lady in question was as indifferent as an Indian
could be, at least in manner.   They all looked at

me for my opinion—the lady excepted. I will
confess that I felt embarrassed, though I had but
half a dozen Indians for my audience. An answer
however was necessary. 'I thank you, my friend,'
said I, 'and needed not this new proof of your
friendship. I am sensible Che-manitou has smiled
upon you; that you are his favourite children.
But we white men have been spoiled by education; we have been taught to think many things
necessary that you red men can do well without;
and inferior as our mode of life is to yours, it is
not the least of its evils that it has unfitted us for
the simple pleasures that Che-manitou every day
gives you. I have friends and a mother far away
towards the rising sun. She does not know the red
men, and might not be a mother to your sister.
Your sister, if I should take her to the rising sun
with me, would pine for her green woods and wigwam by the bright Shiawassee. She will doubtless be happier as she is. She will take for her
husband some red man like yourself, who will love
her, and prize the blessings which Che-manitou
yields you. I again thank you, my friend, and
your sister. I must, after a few days, leave this
country; but I shall bear my friends in my heart,
and in the crowded city where the white men live,
I shall often sigh for these green woods, and lament
the absence of my red friends.'"

LETTER XIV.

Dexter, Washtenaw Co., M. T., Dec. 15th.

I have been waiting here since I last wrote, in order to join an exploring party of three or four individuals, to go up into Shiawassee county, to examine lands. A heavy snow-storm has set in to-day, however, and as it will put an end to the expedition, I shall probably start by myself for the Kalamazoo country to-morrow. The journey to Grand River, which I proposed to myself, I shall, from the time it would consume, be compelled now to abandon entirely. I do not regret the time I have spent here, for I am not far from the centre of the territory; and while I have my head-quarters at a good inn, in a well-settled place, I can, in a ride of a few miles, plunge at once into the wilderness. It is a pretty dangerous matter, however, for a stranger to go without a guide reconnoitring through a country where every hill, lake, and wood looks so much like its brother that the ordinary landmarks are of no assistance to the eye. The scenery of Michigan will be far more attract-

ive when cultivation shall have given variety to a
landscape which, however beautiful at present, is
somewhat monotonous.   After visiting nearly a
dozen of the transparent ponds of every size which
stud the surface of the country, and finding but two
or three whose firm banks of some fifteen or
twenty feet elevation assumed a picturesque appearance, from the irregular manner in which they
pushed their beautifully wooded promontories far
into the lakes they bounded, I started, the other
day, to visit a sheet of water somewhat elevated,
about twelve miles off.   My way, after going a
mile or two from the village, led through oak openings of rolling land, called " the Short Hills," which
I can best assimilate to a collection of enormous
graves—the tombs of households, if you choose—
thrown confusedly together upon a perfectly level
surface ; where a patch of wild meadow-land, a
cranberry marsh, or a bog that looked like the
desolated bed of a lake, and frequently, indeed, the
shallow lake itself, filled up the intervals.   The
huge oaks that crowned the summits of these
formal mounds were the only objects that relieved
the dreariness of the landscape ; even they, I
thought, while riding alone beneath their branches,
that sighed to the December wind, were not the
most enlivening objects in the world.   I rode thus

for miles without seeing a living thing except a raven, which, as that description of bird is only found in those parts of the Union where wolves still infest the country, I at once took it for granted was hovering near one of the savage beasts to which he so faithfully plays the jackal. Wheeling my horse suddenly from the trail towards a thicket of dwarf oaks, where I expected to find the carrion deer that attracts these worthies, he shied from the bush, and I was thrown upon the spot. After extricating the foot, by which I was dragged a yard or two, from the stirrup, I sprang up but little hurt, and moved as quickly as possible to catch my horse, who, having paused for an instant in a clump of trees near by, turned his head round, like a pointer taken aback with the scent after he has passed a bush, and stood calmly gazing at me. At the first step towards the rascal, however, he moved nearly a rod sideways, and then, ducking his head towards the ground, and throwing his heels high in the air, my ungrateful courser, accompanying these motions with every additional mark of disrespect he could summon to his aid, left his master alone in the wilderness. He disappeared behind a hill in a moment. I could not help ejaculating, with the Kentuckian whose house and family had been burned up by the savages, while he was cleaning his rifle at a brook hard by—" This is very *ridiculous*."   No time was to be lost, however.   It was late in the day, and I was far from any house ; while the occasional flakes of snow which began to fall from the black lowering sky, threatened a storm which might cover in a moment the only path that could guide me homeward. I sat down at once among the long dry grass, and stripping off my leggings, and disembarrassing my heels of the now useless spurs, stowed all away in my coat-pockets.   The coat itself I rolled up in a bundle around my left arm, and taking my gun, to which I applied a fresh cap, in my right, I strode off in as good a humour as one could summon under such provoking circumstances.   I could not help thinking, indeed, how much worse matters might have been had I been thus deserted in one of the broad prairies, thirty miles, perhaps, from any house. As for the loss of my horse, I felt so indignant against the inconsiderate brute, that, I confess, it did not much trouble me.   Thus did I trudge on, growing momentarily in better humour with myself.   The scene around was dreary at present ; but having had all the wild flowers that grow in Michigan described to me, I exercised my imagination by conceiving the more attractive appearance it must wear in summer.   I thought how the brown woods must look when the lofty oaks around were clothed in their deep-green foliage. I thought of the various vines and flowers which then fill the broad openings between their stems—of the clumps of cluster-roses that here grow wild and cover whole acres—of the crimson daisy and fragrant balm pink, the deep-hued lichnidia, and gorgeous golden rod, which, with jonquils and amaranth, the purple fox-glove and saffron-coloured silk-weed, paint the surface of the soil. I could fancy the glossy leaves of the nightshade with its white blossoms and poisonous berries, the creeping ivy, and red columbine, clustering at the base of the hills. The snow-white lily of the valley, the lilac-tinted adder's-tongue, and straw-coloured arrow-head, shooting through the long grass between, while the purple fleur-de-lis bloomed along the wet marshes, where the splendid cardinal-flower tossed its scarlet blossoms in the breeze.

I must have practised horticulture in this way for some time when, on rising a slight eminence in my path, I saw my amiable roan standing quietly look-ing in the direction whence I was coming, appa-rently waiting for me. I was completely molli-fied. I forgave him the little freak, and advanced with a light heart to lay my hand upon the bridle. He moved a little, and so did I. He moved a little

more, and I stood still. I spoke to him, but he
continued moving. I coaxed him, in a tone that
would have melted the heart of one of the marble
horses of St. Mark's; he was moved by it—only
farther from me. I whistled to him—(I had taught
him a day or two before to come to my whistle,
when he had obeyed me like a dog)—he stopped,
and I advanced once more to lay my hand on the
saddle, and the scoundrel broke into a trot just as
I was about touching him. I brought my piece to
my shoulder, and could hardly forbear drawing the
trigger upon him as I stood.

The ground now rolled like the waves of a
frozen sea, and my nefarious brute, who soon
began to stalk leisurely along about a hundred
yards ahead of me, would, to carry out the figure,
be just topping the combing while I was in the
trough, and vice versa—like two children balancing on a plank. It was perfectly insufferable,
mile after mile, to see that eternal saddle bobbing
up and down a hundred yards ahead of me. Sometimes, indeed, the vexatious wearer would step
aside among a cluster of oaks, to nip the tender
grass which still lingered around their roots; and
then, as he would arch his neck, and, seeming to
admire the Indian blanket and flame-coloured surcingle which, after the gay taste of the West, I had

buckled, combining use with ornament, to the back of the ungrateful brute, dash off with a snort into a patch of prairie-land, I could not but admire the eye of fire and gracefully-gathering limbs of the spirited creature. I wished, however, that he was anybody's horse but mine, disporting himself at that rate. At last, at a turning of the path he disappeared behind a hill, and ceasing longer to tantalize, left me comparatively comfortable. I reached the first "clearing" about twenty minutes afterward, and looking along the highway which here commenced, my horse was nowhere to be seen. Tired alike with walking and vexation, and parched with thirst (I had neither eaten nor drunk since breakfast, and it was now nightfall), I advanced to the only shantee near, and knocked at the door. There was no answer, and I shook it violently. A rush-bottomed chair rattled, and a cat, the solitary occupant, sprang out through a broken window. I soon found my way, however, to the dilapidated trunk of a large sycamore-tree near, which formed the top of a well, and drawing up a moss-covered bucket, I placed my lips to the rusty iron-bound brim and took a draught, to which the most delicious of Lynch's chateau were but vile *vin-du-pays* in comparison. I can remember but one drink in my life before to compare with it, and that was from a similar goblet, after other lips than mine had hallowed the brim. A few moments after a lad rode into the yard with the object of my pursuit, whose bridle had been broken to pieces in the effort of several men to catch him a mile or two off. I was mounted in a moment, and regained my lodgings in an hour; when I found that the adventure of the day had not impaired my relish for a supper of fresh pike and white-fish, just smoking on the table.

The range of hills which traverse the peninsula longitudinally near here, though never, I believe, more than 150 feet high, are said by some to constitute the most elevated part of Michigan. As they abound in game, and consist altogether of oak openings, you can conceive of nothing more animating than to gallop over them on horseback. I was out again among them yesterday; and having a pocket-compass and a map of the country with me, I ventured to leave the trails that wind among the hollows, and scamper over the hills as my fancy led me. A large flock of grouse rose almost from beneath my horse's feet as I topped the first slight eminence, and then, just as the animal was recovering from the flurry into which the rushing sound of their wings threw him, a tall broad-antlered buck, the largest I ever saw, sprang from a small covert, and bounded through the wide forest glades. Away too I went—the feeling was irresistible—I could see the fellow leaping as if he had wings, over the rolling land, and the clear bracing atmosphere had given spirits to my horse, that sent us ahead like one and the same animal. In spite of the deer's prodigious jumps, which were as high as they were long, I had gained decidedly on the chase, when, coming to the brow of a steep hill, he dashed down the side, and was far away over another before my less agile horse could descend the first. I saw two more deer, besides several flocks of grouse, during my morning's ride. Singularly enough, this was the only time that I had moved a mile without a gun since I left New-York ; and it was the only opportunity I have had to use one to advantage. If Der Freyschutz were in this region, I should certainly let the wild huntsman make his own terms with me for better luck.

To-day, for the first time, I saw the meadows on fire. They are of vast extent, running far into the woods like the friths of a lake ; and as the wild grass, which they supply in the greatest profusion, furnishes the new settler with all the hay he uses for his stock, they are burnt over thus annually to make it tender. These fires, travelling far over the country, seize upon the large prairies, and consuming every tree in the woods, except the hardiest, cause the often-mentioned oak openings, so characteristic of Michigan scenery. It is a beautiful sight to see the fire shooting in every direction over these broad expanses of land, which are kindled at a variety of points. The flame at one moment curls along the ground, and seems to lick up its fuel from below, while at the next it tumbles over like the breakers of the sea upon the dried grass, and sweeps it in a wave of fire from the ground. I found myself repeatedly surrounded by the fire, while riding hither and thither, watching its progress; but was only on two occasions exposed to any inconvenience—once when my horse was bogged to the saddle-girths, so that I had to dismount in a morass, covered with high weeds, to which the flame was approaching, and again when I found myself in a small patch of woodland, which crackled and roared like Tophet itself.

As I rode to and fro here, trying to find a point where, if necessary, I might encounter the flame to the least disadvantage, if unable to avoid it altogether, the ridiculous position in which I had placed myself reminded me not a little of that which Andrew Fairservice occupied on the rock, when he trotted hither and thither on his narrow

platform, to avoid the bullets of Rob Roy's cate-
rans. A finer subject for reflection, however,
presented itself near the spot. A small brook
crossed the meadow, and I bethought myself of
placing it between me and the fire, which was
closing undesirably near around me; but my horse,
when I rode him rapidly to the brink, and endeavoured to jump him, recoiled. I wheeled
round, and tried it again; but his recent expe-
rience in the treacherous marsh made him fear the
sedgy margin, and nothing could prevail upon the
cautious animal to approach it. At the last attempt, he recoiled so suddenly with a terrified
snort, that I was nearly thrown over his head;
and looking for the new cause of anxiety where
the stream wound around, so as almost to double
itself in front of me I saw, on the little peninsula of the burning meadow thus formed, an Indian
standing with folded arms amid the wreathing
smoke, and surveying my motions with an aspect
of perfect calmness. He was a middle-aged man,
rather tall, and in the full costume of his tribe.
The hair on his forehead, which was seamed with
several ghastly scars, was nearly white; but three
long plaited locks of raven black fell down behind,
from the crimson handkerchief which bound his
brows. He wore a white woollen frock, edged

with black, with scarlet leggings and moccasins, while armlets of silver, and a belt containing his tomahawk and scalping-knife, completed his equipments.   All these, however, were observed afterward, when I had given up the attempt to cross the brook, and spurring through the flame where it was lowest, had placed myself by the side of the old warrior.   But. for the present I remained fixed in my seat, gazing on the noble apparition with as much delight as if my own call had evoked it from the ground.   I had seen a dozen Indians, of all sizes and sexes, in the course of the day, not one of whom had awakened the slightest interest; but there was that about the port and bearing of this grim-looking savage which, with the somewhat theatrical attitude he assumed, and the circumstances under which I first beheld him, carried me away completely. He smiled when I approached him, and saluted me with great kindness of manner ; though, as neither of us understood the language of the other, there could be but little interchange of ideas between us.   The few Indian expressions of which I am master were soon expended, and he seemed not to have a word of English to give me in exchange.   He made me understand, however, that the frightful wounds which disfigure his noble

front were received while fighting on the side of
the British against the Americans at Sandusky.

Grass Lake, Jackson Co., M. T., Dec. 16.

The storm of yesterday still prevailed when I
left my excellent quarters at the growing little
hamlet of Dexter, to find my way towards the
country watered by the beautiful *Kekalamazoo*.   I
had been furnished by mine host with a map of the
route for the first eight or ten miles; and it would
have amused you to see me occasionally stopping
in a furious snow-storm to balance my pocket-
compass on the hasty chart thus supplied.   I found
my way, however, with very little difficulty,
through a thick wood, where the heavy coat of
snow that robed the trees gave a most fantastic
appearance to the forest, and about noon I struck
the Washtenaw trail to the west.   The travelling,
however, was any thing but agreeable.   The snow,
being soft, would "ball," as it is called, beneath
my horse's feet, and what with the stumbling and
slipping on this account, I have been unable after
a day's travel to make more than twenty miles.
There was barely light enough left for me to distinguish my way, when I arrived at a comfortable
log-house belonging to an intelligent and hospitable

farmer, a recent emigrant from the western part of the sate of New-York. The owner of the dwelling was absent; and it was not till after a parley of some minutes, between two very pretty women, whom I could distinguish through the window by the light of a tempting-looking fire within, that I gained admittance to pass the night. Once there, however, nothing could exceed the kindness of the family to make the few hours of my sojourn pass agreeable.

Spring-Arbour, Dec. 17.

It snowed when I rose at dawn this morning; but my hospitable entertainer of last night insisted, after an early breakfast, upon accompanying me several miles on my journey; and when he finally parted with me, would not hear of receiving any thing in compensation.

The snow still continues, and the road becoming worse and worse, I have made even less progress to-day. But there is something so wild and picturesque in the country through which I am passing, that even such travelling has its pleasures. I have counted more than a dozen lakes on my route; and though some of them are only dreary-looking pools, covering a few acres, in the midst of an extensive moss-marsh, yet the short sudden hills which surround others, with the beautiful groves of white oak on their banks, and the natural meadows that open upon their mimic friths, make a most romantic appearance. I came unexpectedly upon a travelling band of Ottawas this morning, in one of the most abrupt of these passes. They were returning home amply furnished with presents from the recent treaty held on the Wabash; and their fluttering blankets, gleaming weapons, and gaudy equipments generally, would have made them a fine subject for a painter, as a furious squall of snow swept along the side-hill they were descending. We exchanged the customary salutation, "Boju" (probably from the French bonjour), and passed on.

There are several Indian graves immediately before the door of the shantee where I am stopping for the night, which I am told are regularly visited and weeded by the surviving relatives of those here buried. My host has had the good taste to put a fence around them, to keep his cattle from the spot—a piece of attention with which the Indians appeared to be much gratified at their last visit; and I may here observe that the settlers of Michigan, generally, appear to treat this ill-fated race with a degree of kindness and consideration that might well be imitated in other sections of our frontier. This morning I crossed the far-flowing Washtenong, or Grand River, near the new village of Jacksonburg; and the sight of its clear smooth waters inspired a new regret, that I must abandon my original intention of following them down to the last trading-post.

Forks of the Kekalamazoo (Calhoun), Dec. 18.

This never-ending storm still continues, and the trails, where not incessantly travelled, being now completely covered and effaced, I lost my way this morning, and wandered several miles from the track. After traversing a broad marsh, however, where my horse seemed loth enough to venture, I struck a burr-oak opening, and found my way by the *blazed** trees back to the main trail. A man who is used to it, I am told, can get along very well in this way ; but you can imagine, that where one has frequently to cross openings of some two or three hundred yards in width, and then hunt up these primitive guide-posts, which only occur at long intervals, and have their slice of bark taken out at either side, it is not quite so easy to find his way here, especially with the snow blowing full in his face, as if walking through the rectangular streets of Phila-

* " Blazed" trees are marked with an axe or hatchet, to designate that a trail runs near them.

delphia.   It took me three hours to gain six miles in
this way, my horse slipping and floundering at almost every step.   But, lost as I was, I could not help
pausing frequently when I struck the first burr-oak
opening I had ever seen, to admire its novel beauty.
It looked more like a pear-orchard than any thing
else to which I can assimilate it—the trees being
somewhat of the shape and size of full-grown pear-
trees, and standing at regular intervals apart from
each other on the firm level soil, as if planted by
some gardener.   Here, too, I first saw deer in
herds; and half-frozen and weary as I was, the
sight of those spirited-looking creatures sweeping
in troops through these interminable groves, where
my eye could follow them for miles over the smooth
snowy plain, actually warmed and invigorated me,
and I could hardly refrain from putting the rowels
into my tired horse, and launching after the noble
game.

What a country this is.   Into land like this,
which is comparatively undervalued by those seek-
ing to settle on the prairie, a man can run his plough
without felling a tree; and, planting a hundred
acres, where he would clear but ten in the unsettled
districts of New-York, raise his twenty-five bushels
of wheat to an acre in the very first season.   "How
is the soil here, sir?" said I to a farmer whose broad

fields, though but a year under cultivation, looked as if they had been tilled for ten. "A pretty good gravelly loam of eighteen inches; but I think some of moving off to Kalamazoo, where they have it *four feet deep, and so fat that it will grease your fingers.*" Railroads and canals will make one broad garden of Michigan; and even now there is something singularly pleasing to light upon spots in the wildest districts which, were it not for the rude shantees which indicate their recent settlement,— often of but a few months back,—might be mistaken for the cultivated farms of an old country. The absence of stumps in the land under cultivation, and the open groves adjacent, give a smiling openness to the landscape which, with the myriads of wild flowers that brighten the woods in their season, must make the aspect of the country perfectly delightful. I hardly know, though, how some of your city *élégants*, the votaries of Delmonico, or the fair visitants at Gardiner's, would meet the inconveniences of travelling here. As for eating, indeed, they might manage with the aid of cranberry sauce to rough it on venison and wild honey, backed by the finest potatoes and best wheat bread in the world; but I think that, when it comes to sleeping, they would be somewhat posed between a bed in the bush and one shared with the hospitable inmates of a cabin, whose dormitory for the whole family is often, as well as their kitchen and parlour, comprised in a single room. Were it not an infraction of the laws of hospitality, I could draw some queer pictures of scenes I have witnessed in this way.

I have now passed the central region where the Eastern and Western rivers of Michigan have their rise; and while I follow down the pebbly waters of the beautiful Kekalamazoo to their western outlet, and from thence pass to the mouth of the St. Joseph's, you must not expect the same regularity in my correspondence that I have hitherto attempted to preserve.

LETTER XV.

Marshall, Calhoun Co., M. T., Dec.

I confess that it was with some pleasure that—after dividing my time for several days, as described in my last, between roads rendered almost impassable by continual snows and log-cabins, where the recent settler, however hospitable, had but spare accommodation to offer to the passing traveller—on rising an elevation on the northern bank of the Kekalamazoo, I saw a large frame-building, which was evidently an inn, rearing its comfortable-looking chimneys above a group of log-huts on the plain beneath. My horse, who had doubtless repented of former escapades in the companionable intercourse which had now for some time subsisted between us, seemed to sympathize in the feeling; and pricking up his ears, as he snuffed the grain in a flour-mill directly beneath us, we descended the slippery height, and were soon tolerably well-housed in the new inn of Marshall. The house was, indeed, not as yet plaistered inside; and the different bed-rooms, though lathed, seemed divided from each other by lines rather imaginary than real; but the bar-room wore already the insignia of a long-established inn in an old community; and apprized me at once, by the placarded sheriffs' notices and advertisements for stolen horses, grain to be sold, and labourers wanted, which indicate the growth of business in country life, that society was in a pretty mature state—at least six months old—in the county town of Marshall. I was, therefore, not at all surprised to find among these notices a call for "a railroad meeting" in the evening, especially as nearly eighteen months had elapsed since the first white man erected his cabin in this section of the country.

The meeting, which might be termed a crowded one, was conducted with more animation than unanimity. There were several intelligent men present, however; and I listened with interest to their exposition of the resources of this section of Michigan, which, as a wheat growing country, may be justly compared to the celebrated Genessee valley of New-York, while the soil, as I have heard it well observed by a resident, "unlike the heavily-timbered land of the Eastern States, instead of wearing out one generation in subduing it for the purposes of the husbandman, invites the plough at once." Nor, if a rail-road should be constructed from Detroit to the mouth of the St. Joseph's passing through the counties of Wayne, Washtenaw, Jackson, Calhoun, Kalamazoo, Van Buren, and Berrien, do I think it would be too bold to assert that the amount to be transported by the time the work was completed would be equal to one million of barrels, which is a less estimate by two hundred thousand than I have seen given by an intelligent writer on this subject in a Detroit paper. The route thus designated, I am persuaded, is the right one for a rail-road; though, should a different mode of communication be determined upon, it would be difficult to decide whether it were most expedient to construct a canal from the falls of Grand River to Detroit, or from the navigable waters of the St. Joseph's to Monroe. I do not hesitate to add, that before two years have expired, all of these routes will be under contract. The abundant resources of Michigan are developing so rapidly, that they will shortly require all these outlets; and in a country where you may drive a barouche-and-four for hundreds of miles in any direction through the woods, the expense of constructing more artificial ways will be comparatively trivial.

Did I not know how ignorant generally the

people of the east are of the resources and condition of this country, it would surprise me that
some New-York capitalists have not embarked
in some of these works. A tempting speculation
might be realized by laying out a rail-road on one
of these routes above described; having first purchased the land in its vicinity at government prices,
to be disposed of afterward when its value should
be enhanced by the completion of different sections
of the work. The ingenious writer, above alluded
to, has already suggested this mode of covering the
expense of such an undertaking. You can have
no idea of the feeling existing on the subject of internal communications throughout Michigan; and
it would amuse you not a little to witness the
heart-burnings and jealousies on the subject which
pervade a country but just beginning to be peopled. The rapidity with which people establish
themselves and collect the indications of agricultural wealth around them, before they have even
the ordinary comforts of life, will, in a great measure, account for their looking thus ahead and
quarrelling about the game before it is hunted
down. The farmer, who has more grain in the
sheaf stacked in the field than he can accommo-
date in his barn, is naturally more eager to find the
means of sending a share of it to market.

I was quite diverted at the turn matters took at the meeting which suggested these remarks, when a discussion in relation to the various routes to be recommended to government in case they should consent to make a railroad through the Peninsula, became unpleasantly warm. "This pother reminds me, Mr. Chairman," said an old pioneer, " of two trappers who, in planning a spearing expedition for the next day, quarrelled about the manner in which a turtle, which they proposed taking, should be cooked for their supper, after the day's sport was over. An old Indian happily settled the difficulty, by proposing that they should first *catch the turtle!* Now, sir, as this railroad,"—'the case is not at all parallel'—interrupted a still more ancient speaker, "for *Nature* has already caught the turtle for us. She meant the railroad to pass right along here, and nowhere else."

The councils of the meeting were not on the whole so harmonious as I could have wished from the courtesies offered me after its termination by the adherents of the two parties of Guelphs and Ghibbelines, which distract the unhappy city of Marshall; but it was surprising to a stranger, upon looking round at the hovels of mud and logs which as yet occupy its site, to find so many persons of intelligence and refinement thus collected within their precincts. The population of Michigan generally, —as I believe I have before observed,—is much superior in character to the ordinary settlers of a new country. The ease with which a man can here support a family as a farmer, induces a great many persons of all professions, in other states, to abandon their former pursuits and become tillers of the soil. The alteration of life, I should judge by the contentment I everywhere witness, is almost always for the better.

I have met with several dispeptics who have been completely cured of that horrible disease by their change of life. With such, health is a sensation—a positive delight; and in duly estimating the blessing, they of course were ever ready to praise the conditions upon which they enjoy it. Others again, bred up in a city, find in the indulgence of that love of rural life which, when it is a natural taste, is inextinguishable, an ample compensation for breaking up established habits and associations. The majority again are men of slender means; and while the necessity of attending practically to the subsistence of their families keeps them employed, the want of pecuniary resources prevents their embarking in the thousand idle schemes which tend so often to the chagrin and the ruin of "gentlemen farmers." But the main cause of Michigan being settled by such respectable people remains yet to be mentioned. It is, that no one can take up an acre of land without first paying cash for it, at one of the three land-offices of the territory. The whole surface of the Peninsula has either been, or is now being, surveyed into townships of six miles square. These again are sub-divided into sections of a mile square; which sections are again cut up into lots of forty acres; which is the smallest quantity of land that can be taken up from the government. The price is invariably $1 25 an acre. When you consider, therefore, that every emigrant who means to *locate* (this is a sound American word, and as indispensable in the vocabulary of a western man as are an axe and a rifle among his household furniture), must, however poor, have some earnings in advance to purchase the spot upon which he is to live, and to bring his family to such a remote distance, it will be easy to conceive that the industrious and the enterprising must constitute the largest portion of such a population of freeholders. The prosperity of a whole community, composed of such aggregate masses, may be safely predicted; and though one sometimes meets with those whom the first process of accumulating renders discontented, and induces to speak ill of the country, yet in general I may say, that the pride of a Michiganian, in the beautiful land of his adoption, is as strong as the home-feeling upon which the citizens of some of the older States pique themselves. As for the sickness which always prevails more or less among the new settlers, to one who is aware of their imprudences the wonder is that the majority of them escape with their lives. Think but of people setting themselves down on a soil of twenty inches in depth, and in the month of June, when the weeds and wild flowers o'ertop the head of the tallest man, turning over the rank soil immediately around their dwellings, and allowing the accumulation of vegetable decomposition to be acted upon by a vertical sun, and steam up for months under their very nostrils; and yet this, I am told, is continually practised by settlers who come in late in the season, and are anxious still to have a crop the first year. Here, as in the case of those settlers who, for the sake of the wild hay, locate themselves near the great marshes, imprudence alone is manifested ; but the charge of culpability will justly attach to some other cases, when nuisances, not before existing, are created by the owners of property. I allude to the practice, expressly prohibited by the laws of Michigan, of flooding land while constructing mill-ponds, without removing the green timber growing upon the spot. So pernicious is this to the health of the neighbourhood, that it affects very sensibly the value of property near the new pond; and yet, in their eagerness to have mills erected, and aid the market of their overflowing granaries, the new inhabitants overlook entirely the gross violation of their laws, and the melancholy consequences which ensue to their families. Another cause of sickness is drinking the water of springs or rivers which rise in marshes, and are of course impregnated with their baleful properties, instead of digging wells where water is not liable to such exception. As for general healthfulness of situation, I believe it is agreed that the banks of the small lakes which so abound in the peninsula are—when these transparent bodies of water are surrounded by a sand-beach, which is the case with about a third of them—among the healthiest. They are fed generally by deep springs, and in many instances are supposed to have a subterranean outlet; while so beautifully transparent are their waters, that the canoe suspended on their bosom seems to float in mid-air. These lakes abound with fish; and in some of them, of only a few acres in extent, fish have been taken of forty pounds weight. They generally lie imbosomed in the oak openings, and with their regular and almost formal banks crowned with open groves, these silver pools might be readily taken for artificial trout-ponds in a cultivated park. I need hardly add, that it is necessary to diverge, as I have, from the route generally travelled, to see these scenic gems, so numerous, lonely, and beautiful. Not one in a hundred has a settler on its banks; and I confess I take a singular pleasure in surveying these beauties, as yet unmarred by the improving axe of the woodman, and unprofaned by the cockney eyes of city tourists; nor would I change my emotions, while ranging alone over the broad meadows, traversing the lofty forests, or loitering by the limpid lakes of Michigan, for the proudest musings of the scholar who revels in classic land. It may argue a want of refinement in taste, but I confess that a hoary oak is to me more an object of veneration than a mouldering column; and that I would rather visit scenes where a human foot has never trod than dwell upon those gilded by the most arrogant associations of our race.

What are the temples which Roman robbers have reared,—what are the towers in which feudal oppression has fortified itself,—what the blood-stained associations of the one, or the despotic superstitions of the other, to the deep forests which the eye of God has alone pervaded, and where Nature, in her unviolated sanctuary, has for ages laid her fruits and flowers on his altar! What is the echo of roofs that a few centuries since rung with barbaric revels, or of aisles that pealed the anthems of painted pomp, to the silence which has reigned in these dim groves since the first fiat of Creation was spoken!

I shall diverge from my western course to-morrow a few miles southward, in order to visit a group of lakes, near which a band of Pottawattamies, a tribe I have not yet seen, have their encampment. I will leave this letter open, in order to give you the result of my visit.

Calhoun Co., M. T., Dec. 23.

I write to you from a little cottage in a beautiful grove, not far from the banks of the Kekalamazoo, where two young gentlemen, recently from the east, have made their home in this land of enterprise. It is amusing to observe how little singularity people here attach to a mode of life which, in older countries, would be looked upon as highly eccentric. My entertainers are both young lawyers, liberally educated, and unused to privation; and yet the house in which I am passing the night, with every article of furniture it contains, is of their own manufacture; a saw, an axe, a wood-knife, and a jack-plane being their only tools. It would amuse you not a little to look through the window, and see our group at this moment. One of my companions, whose axe and rifle are suspended by wooden hooks to the rafters over his head, is professionally engaged in drawing a declaration at the table upon which I am writing; while the other, having just got through removing the remains of our game dinner, prepared and cooked by his chum, is now sitting with a long pipe in his mouth, watching a coffee-pot, which steams up so fragrantly from the live embers, that no light consideration would induce me to part with the interest I have in its contents. Their house, which has been thus occupied for three months, is a perfect pattern of neatness; though, as it consists of but a single room, no little ingenuity is required to arrange their books, house-keeping apparatus, and sporting equipments, so as to preserve even an appearance of order in such a bandbox. They have already sufficient business, they tell me, to sustain their moderate household; and as the Indians supply them with abundance of provisions, they have ample leisure to devote to study.

It is not very uncommon, however, to meet thus

with persons of education, and some accomplishment, under as humble a roof as this in the wilds of Michigan. For so rapid is the growth of society here, that he who aims at a prominent station in the new community must be a pioneer far in advance of the growing settlements. Two years ago the first white man raised his log hut in the county of Calhoun; it has now a population of 1500, and I have passed an evening in at least one mud-plastered cabin, whose fair and elegant inmates would grace any society.

When I see the wives and daughters of men habituated by early education to all the comforts of refined life, thus submitting cheerfully to every privation for the sake of those whose happiness is involved with theirs, I cannot help calling to mind the jargon of novels so often adopted by people of sense in cities, where the terms " excellent match," and " supporting in the station where she has been accustomed to move," usurp all considerations of mutual affection, and capability in the parties united to study each other's happiness through life. I am more than ever persuaded that there are two kinds of refinement in life, which bear but little similarity to each other; and the one least often met with is that which is independent of modes and fashions, of tailors, milliners, and cabinet-makers,—which does not necessarily lean upon a pier-table, nor repose upon a *chaise longue*,—which—shall I confess it ?— may be nursed without a silver fork. The purest porcelain which the factories of China produce does not require a single tint upon its surface to show the fineness of the texture; but that in which coarser clay is blended is always charged with some gaudy hue to hide the intermixture of the mongrel material. This doctrine, though, is so little in accordance with those taught in those English novels which constitute the modern text-books of elegance, that while the mode of eating an egg is the test of good-breeding, and the art of pattering French phrases the criterion of intellectual cultivation, I should as soon think of interfering with the particular province of a lackey or *friseur*, as of breaking a spear at such disadvantage with the authors of " Almack's" and " Men and Manners—".

But a truce to this prosing. Did you ever see a *jumper ?* A couple of hickory poles so bent that the runners and shafts are of the same piece, with a crate placed on four props, complete this primitive species of sledge ; and when the crate is filled with hay, and the driver well wrapped-up in a buffalo robe, the " turn-out" is about as comfort-

able a one as a moderate man could wish.   In such
a vehicle as this, with a harness every way suitable, viz. a collar of undressed deerskin and reins
of rope (the twisted bark of trees is often used),
did I, with one of my present entertainers, the first
companion I have yet had in travelling, sally out
from Marshall this morning.   My horse, who had
detained me there a couple of days by a soreness
of his back proceeding from the saddle, seemed
highly to approve of this new mode of travel:
Mr. Osbaldistone behind Tom Thumb, Sesostris
in his chariot, or *Yorke* in one of Brower's new
omnibuses, could not have dashed off with more
glee than did we with our merry jumper along the
dimpling waters of the Kekalamazoo; when, lo!
just as we had crossed a bridge of unhewn timber,
and were under full way through the oak openings,
our frail bark struck on a rock hidden by the snow,
and we were capsized and wrecked in an instant.
Fortunately, though both were pitched like a couple
of quoits from the machine, we were neither of us
hurt; and my companion returning to the settlement to borrow a horse, I mounted mine, and
leaving the remains of my crank establishment
where chance had thrown them, I rode on, while
he overtook me in time to introduce me to his
friend, and make me so pleasantly at home in their

dwelling as, you must observe, I now am. Good-night; I will tell you to-morrow evening how we dispose of our time till then.

December 24th.

The air was mild this morning, and large flocks of snow-birds twittering among the bur-oaks, with jays screaming from the woods, and packs of grouse rising continually before us in the open-ings, made our route to the camp of Warpkesick, a Pottawattamie chieftain,* more like a ride in the spring-time than a winter excursion. I was ac-companied by my companion of yesterday; and as we were both well-mounted, we galloped over the openings towards Lyon Lake, at a rate that brought us in a few minutes to the white sand-beach which fringes that beautiful water. The marks of an Indian trail were here easily discerni-ble; and following the foot-marks dashed in the yielding sand, the frequent print of moccasins soon led us again away from the shore into a tall wood beyond. A morass, that shook for yards around as our horses' hoofs encountered 'the sagging peat, was next to be crossed; and then passing between two small lonely-looking lakes, where a tall pine or two lifted its sweeping cone above the

* See note E.

tapering tamaracks around, we struck at last into a dense forest. Here the numerous deer-runways, with the flocks of wild turkeys, and innumerable tracks of rackoons, wolves, and bears, showed us that we were upon a favourite hunting-ground of the Pottawattamies. As for the wolves, they are little disturbed by the Indians, who consider them fair hunters like themselves, and privileged to go unmolested. They generally abound around a hunting-camp; and soon grow fat on the offals of game slaughtered near it. But bears, though the successful hunter invariably takes his dead quarry by the paw, calls him his grandfather, and asks his pardon for killing him, " being compelled to it by necessity,"* are hunted with great avidity; and you generally find a tamarack swamp, the favourite covert of these animals, in the vicinity of a hunting-camp.

We had ridden for about a mile through the heavily timbered land, when reaching the banks of the Nottawaseepe, a branch of the St. Joseph's, I heard the sound of children's voices, and descried two or three red urchins wading through the shallow stream on stilts, while others of a similar age were amusing themselves in shooting bows and arrows on the opposite side. We immediately forded the

* See note F.

stream, and making our way into a swamp, where the horses sank to the knee at every step, came unexpectedly upon a piece of firm ground, some eighty yards in diameter, and found ourselves in the middle of the camp of Warpkesick. It was composed of three or four wigwams only, but they were large, and probably contained several families each. They were constructed of mats, arranged precisely in the form of a tent,* and supported in the same manner, an opening being left in the centre for the escape of the smoke, and a blanket suspended over a hole cut in the side, supplying the place of a door. The day being mild for the season of the year, the indwellers of these simple habitations were, at the moment of our arrival, variously occupied in several groups on the outside. Some of the men were cleaning their weapons, and others were arranging a bundle of muskrat traps ; while one old fellow, whose screwed-up features, peering from under a mass of grizzly locks, indicated the cunning of the trapper, rather than the boldness of the hunter, was occupied in flaying an otter but just taken. The women alone, however, appeared to

* The Ottawas have a somewhat different form for their wigwams. See note G.

be assiduously engaged—the men having all a lounging air of indolence, incompatible with the idea of actual employment: pressing skins was the occupation of the former ; and they sat grouped each like a hare in its form around a collection of boiling kettles, over which the skins were suspended.

A tall virago of fifty, whose erect stature, elf locks, and scarlet blanket floating about her person would entitle her to flourish as Meg Merrilies in the frontispiece of Guy Mannering, stood up in the midst ; and had it not been for some tolerably pretty faces among her junior colaborators, might have been taken for Hecate herself, surrounded by the weird sisters of the caldron. A pack of wolfish-looking curs, about twenty in number, completed the assemblage ; which, when you take into consideration the variously coloured calico dresses and wampum ornaments in which the females had arrayed themselves, with the white, blue, red, and green blankets in which the men were wrapped, constituted about as motley a collection as ever followed Falstaff to the field. Warpkesick himself, the chief of the gipsy band, issued from his lodge while I was thus studying the appearance of his adherents. He was a young man, not more than thirty, with a handsome though somewhat voluptuous cast of countenance and remarkably fine eyes. His stature was rather below the middle size ; and though the upper part of his person was extremely well formed, with a deep chest and broad flat shoulders, one of his legs, whether from deformity or misfortune I did not like to inquire, was so twisted under his body as to be worse than useless. He supported himself upon an ashen staff about eight feet in length, and terminating at the bottom in a round ball, to prevent it, probably, from sinking too deeply into the earth while in rapid pursuit of game ; the chief being, in spite of the unsightly encumbrance he is compelled to drag after him, when bounding like a stricken panther on his prey, one of the keenest hunters of his tribe. He received us courteously, but remained standing ; while several Indians gathered in a few moments around him : after shaking hands with them all in succession, I took up a loaded gun, and by way of breaking up the formality of the meeting, desired an eagle-eyed young Indian to make a shot with it. He hesitated for a moment to comply, and immediately all the others, from some whim or other, insisted that I should shoot. Our conversation being altogether in signs, it was some moments before I understood their gestures ; and I confess, that having but little practice with a single ball, I was any thing but unembarrassed when I came to understand the purport of the request they were proffering with so much animation. A small blaze that was instantly made with a tomahawk in a sapling, forty or fifty yards distant, left me no excuse for pretending longer to misunderstand my worthy acquaintances; and placing the gun to my shoulder, I was as much surprised at putting the ball within a couple of inches of the centre, as if the tree had screamed when thus pierced by my random bullet.

Having met with those in Michigan who will drive a rusty nail with a rifle at this distance, and shoot leaves from each other's heads at six rods, I could not account for the degree of approval manifested by the spectators, till my companion informed me that the Indians, owing perhaps to the inferiority of their rifles, which are of English manufacture, are but indifferent marksmen at still objects. " *Tai-ya,*" cried the women, " *Neshin,*" said the chief, and " *Nesheshin,*" echoed his attendants; while the blankets of the lodges were now for the first time raised, and entering, we stretched ourselves on mats around the fire. A youth of nineteen sprang to his feet as I removed the dingy curtain which formed the door, and revealed a face and form that might be the model of an

Apollo. Being ill at the time, he was but half-dressed; the purple blanket dropping from his shoulders setting off a neck and chest of the finest manly proportions. His features were copied by Nature from a Greek model; while his shaven crown, with the single chivalric scalp-lock tufted with a heron's feather, would, in its noble developments, have thrown the disciples of Gall and Spurzheim into ecstasy. The peculiarity of his head-dress, with the beautifully beaded leggins round his ankles, revealed to me at once that the young gentleman was an Indian dandy—a Pottawattamie Pelham in an undress; and I assure you that Mr. C—— never schooled any of his New-York rivals to wear their Spanish cloak with a better air than was exhibited by my red friend Mitosway-Coquatchegun, or Ten-Garters, as he gathered the folds of his blankets about his person.

Pipes were now lit, and Ten-Garters, who was too unwell to smoke himself, politely, after a few whiffs, tendered me his, while my companion, who could partially speak the language, was supplied from another quarter: we were soon perfectly at home. I had picked up from the floor of the lodge, on entering, a rude musical instrument—a species of flute, of imperfect tones, but having a rich mellow sound—when, as I was trying to squeeze a tune from the gammutless pipe, Warpkesick rose abruptly, and stating that he had to start at once on a trapping expedition, signified that we should take our departure. An Indian pony stood at the door, and leaping at one bound into the wooden saddle, an immense bundle of steel-traps was handed to the chief by a by-stander; and accompanied by an Indian on foot, almost as sorry-looking as the miserable beast he rode, our abrupt host disappeared at once into the woods. I was lingering behind to purchase the flute, and had conciliated the squaws wonderfully by tearing out the silk lining of my frock-coat, and giving it in shreds to their children, when my friend, being already mounted, told me we had better move off. I had barely time to cross the saddle, when a whoop rang through the woods, which, while it made my horse spring almost from beneath me, would have wakened Rip Vanwinkle from his twenty years' doze. The piercing cry from the forest was echoed with an exulting shout from every wigwam. A dozen dusky figures leaped through their flimsy porches, with as many rifles gleaming in their hands. He of the heron feather was the first that caught my eye, and as his gun pointed in the direction whence the first whoop came, immediately behind me, I could not help, in spite of the undesirable propinquity of its muzzle, admiring the eagle-eye and superb attitude of the young warrior. Not a soul advanced three paces from the covert whence he sprung. There was a dead silence. The children held their breath, and " Meg Merrilies," who had stepped on a fallen tree at the first outcry, now stood so still that her eldritch form, were it not for the elf locks streaming over her scarlet blanket in the breeze, might have been mistaken for a figure of stone. Another whoop, and the cause of all the commotion at once appeared. A noble buck, roused from his lair by Warpkesick, comes bounding by the camp, and buries his proud antlers in the dust in a moment. A dozen scalping-knives pierce his leathern coat, and the poor creature is stripped of his skin almost before he has time to pant out his expiring breath.

I rode home reflecting upon all I had ever read of the want of vivacity and fire in the Indian character, and concluded that I would rather have witnessed the spirited scene I have just attempted to describe to you, than double all the knowledge I have h therto laid up from such sources.

I leave this comfortable house in the morning, and it will be long before I reach again one half so agreeable.

LETTER XVI.

Prairie Ronde, Kalamazoo Co., M. T., Dec. 26.

"Stranger, will you take a cocktail with us?" called out a tall athletic fellow to me as I was making my way through a group of wild-looking characters assembled an hour since around the fire by which I am now writing. There was a long-haired " hoosier" from Indiana, a couple of smart-looking " suckers"* from the southern part of Illinois, a keen-eyed leather-belted "badger" from the mines of Ouisconsin, and a sturdy yeoman-like fellow, whose white capot, Indian moccasins, and red sash proclaimed, while he boasted a three years' residence, the genuine *wolverine*, or naturalized Michiganian. Could one refuse to drink with such a company? The spokesman was evidently a " red-horse" from Kentucky, and nothing was wanting but a " buck-eye" from Ohio to render the assemblage as complete as it was select. I was in the midst of the first real prairie I had

* So called after the fish of that name, from his going up the river to the mines, and returning at the season when the sucker makes its migrations.

ever seen—on an island of timber, whose lee, while
making slow headway for the last two hours, with
a biting breeze on my beam, it had been my whole
object, aim, and ambition to get—a comfortable
bar-room, a smoking "cocktail," a worshipful
assemblage (Goldsmith's Club was a fool to it) had
never entered my dreams! Could I refuse to
drink with such a company? The warm glass is
in my frozen fingers. The most devout temperance man could see no harm in that! It is touched
smartly by the rim of the red-horse,—it is brushed
by the hooshier,—it rings against the badger,—
comes in companionable contact with the wolverine,—"My respects to you, gentlemen, and luck
to all of us."

Here was a capital commencement with just
the sort of sallad of society I have been long wishing to meet with, having as yet only tasted its
component parts in detail. But auspicious as was
the beginning, I nearly got into a difficulty with
my new acquaintances a few moments afterward,
by handing the landlord a share of the reckoning;
and I took back the coin forced upon me, with many
apologies upon my part for having presumed to
pay part of a "general treat," while labouring
under the disqualifications of being a stranger.
Room was then civilly made for me by the

fireplace, and accepting a pipe proffered by one of the company, a few whiffs made me sufficiently sick and at home to lay it by without further ceremony. "There's *a smart chance of cigars* there in the bar, stranger, if you'd try some of them," said one of the hooshiers.—"Yes," echoed the other; "and they are a heap better than those pipes."—"I allow," rejoined another of the company; "but I wish that fellow would shut the door; he must think that we were all raised in a saw-mill, and then he looks so *peert* whenever he comes in." —"Poor fellow!" ejaculated one who had not yet spoken, "he is considerably troubled with youngness."

"From the eastern side, stranger?" said another to me, "I am told it's tolerable frog pasture. Now here the soil's so deep one can't raise any long sarce—they all get pulled through the other side. We can winter our cows, however, on wooden clocks, there's so many Yankees among us," &c.

A scattering conversation was kept up in similar quaint expressions for some time; but as Mr. Hackett has already given the cream of western phraseology in his whimsical caricature of "the Kentuckian," I will not tire you with enumerating more of those which fell under my observation.

These unique terms, indeed, were poured out so copiously, that it was impossible for one's memory, though elastic as a pair of saddle-bags, to retain them. At last a *train* and a couple of carioles drove up to the door, and I discovered, upon their bundling merrily into these vehicles, that the whole company were bound for a wedding. "Jim," cried one driver to another, snapping his whip, "let our horses run near the silk." *Jim* cracked his snapper, and the light carioles taking the lead, the more humble train skimmed rapidly after them: their dark shadows were soon lost upon the moonlit prairie, and the sound of their bells died away in the distance by the time I had regained my now solitary seat by the fire.

I have had but a sorry time since leaving the agreeable company I spoke of in my last. To-day, indeed, the weather, though cold and windy, has been clear. But on the two previous, I rode for the whole time through alternate snow and sleet, which the wind at times blew so directly in my face as to make it almost impossible to proceed. In one instance, while making my way through a dense forest of twelve or fourteen miles between the openings, without a cabin by the way, my horse stopped suddenly, and looking about ten paces ahead, I saw a couple of deer standing immediately in my path, and gazing on me with the most perfect unconcern; but my fingers were so numb with cold that I was unable to cock my gun, while the timid creatures slowly retired within the depths of the forest. The Kekalamazoo wound through this wood, but the under-growth of timber was so very heavy that its waters, though within a few yards of me, were rarely discernible; and their ample flow, when seen as now swollen by the troubled current of Battle Creek and other tributaries, though capable of bearing boats of considerable burthen, possessed less charms for me than when I first struck the slender rill as it leaped unsullied from its virgin fountain, and went singing on its course. Still it was with regret, when at last ferried over the Kekalamazoo, so long my only companion, that, on turning my horse's head to the south, I took leave of its Arcadian banks for ever. I passed the previous night at the little hamlet of Comstock, where an enterprising young gentleman, after whom the place is called, having the advantage of a good mill-site, is creating a flourishing establishment around him; a frame-store and several log-cabins, with two or three mills, already giving some importance to the situation in a new country. My ride of to-day, having started late, brought me, about sunset, a distance of twenty miles, to the verge of Prairie Ronde ; the intermediate country consisting partly of burr-oak plains, broken sometimes by the short round hills I have before described, and partly of broad grassy meadows, running sometimes into marshes, and occasionally watered by some clear stream, whose sandy bottom would contrast strongly with its low sedgy brink. The ground became higher and firmer as I approached Prairie Ronde ; and then, after riding for a few miles through the openings, when I expected to descend upon a broad meadow, somewhat resembling the many I have seen in Michigan, fully answering to my preconceived ideas of a prairie, I came suddenly upon an immense piece of cleared table-land, some fifty feet above a pretty lake in its vicinity. The scattering houses around its borders, with the island of timber in the centre and the range of six or seven miles of prairie on every side, assured me that this was Prairie Ronde ; while the piercing blast which, as the sun sunk redly on the opposite side, rushed out from his western resting-place and blew the snow-drift in my teeth, made me eager to cross the waste as rapidly as possible, and sufficiently accounts for the pleasure with which I entered this hospitable inn. The collection of houses which stand sheltered by this wood is called " Schoolcraft." The wood itself, though only five or six hundred acres in extent, has a small lake in the centre, and the village, if not the whole settled part of the prairie, is distinguished by the number of fine running-horses, blooded dogs, and keen sportsmen it has in proportion to the population. Fox-hunting on horseback, with full packs of hounds, is the favourite sport; though wolf, bear, and badger-baiting have each their active followers. The soil is so easy of culture and so generous in its product, that the settlers, after attending to their necessary avocations, have ample leisure for their many recreations. Prairie Ronde, though, like all parts of Michigan, in a great measure settled by emigrants from the State of New-York, is said to count a still greater number of its residents from natives of the south and west. The population generally was, perhaps, fairly represented at the assembly to which I so unceremoniously introduced you at the opening of the letter.

Niles, Berrien Co., M. T., Dec. 28.

I have been now for two days in St. Joseph's county, considered among the finest in Michigan; having, since I wrote the above, traversed the counties of St. Joseph and Cass, watered by the St. Joseph's river, which is the most imposing-looking stream I have yet seen. A ride of fourteen miles from Prairie Ronde brought me first to its banks, which, rising occasionally fifty or sixty feet above the water in a sudden bluff, look higher than those of any river I have yet seen in the peninsula. You must already have gathered, from my attempts at portraying Michigan scenery, that neither the grand, the picturesque—hardly even the romantic—are to be numbered among its characteristics. "The beautiful" comprehends them all : and yet you can readily imagine that, that beauty is neither tame nor monotonous which can shine through the dreary months of winter, and make the half-frozen and solitary traveller almost forget its rigours. It is true, that one brought up in a more rugged and broken country might often miss the mountain-tops leaning against the sky,—might sigh for the sound of a cascade, and long once more to plant his foot upon a cliff; and yet, where would the eye more delight to wander than through these beautiful groves, which in summer must stretch their green arcades on every side ? Where rest more happily than on those grassy meadows on which their vistas open ? These streams, too, that sparkle so brightly over their golden beds, are they no substitute for the rushing torrents of more mountainous countries? or does the lichen-covered crag tempt one's footsteps more than this teeming soil, when nature has carpeted it

with the myriad of wild flowers which the summer's
sun calls forth ?   To no scenery of our country that
I have yet seen is the term " Arcadian" more ap-
plicable, than to the rich and fairy landscape on the
western side of the peninsula, watered by the Kekalamazoo and the St. Joseph's.

The latter stream, when I first beheld it, was
filled with floating ice, which the deep and rapid
tide brought down with such force, that my horse
recoiled with affright when I attempted to urge
him into the current, at a point where an old woman
told me was the usual place of fording.   A rope-
ferry, a quarter of a mile farther on, removed the
difficulty; and finding my way along a rich bottom,
where the trail was so encumbered with vines that
it was difficult, even at this season, to keep it, I
hailed a grim-looking Charon, with a shock head of
hair, attired in a green hunting-shirt, who was
standing in the doorway of a cabin on the opposite side, and crossing for me in his scow, I was
soon conveyed across the wintry torrent.   The
country now became gradually more populous
as I approached the village and prairie of White
Pigeon.   I had ridden fourteen miles in the
morning without seeing the sign of a habita-
tion ; and as one meets with neither travellers nor emigrants at this season, there is some

company even in the smoke of a chimney, though you do not stop to warm your fingers by the fire beneath it. I expected long before this to have fallen in with a most agreeable companion, in a gentleman of the country whom I met with at Detroit, and who is a considerable proprietor on the St. Joseph's. Having a fine taste for natural scenery, and being one of the best rifle-shots that I have ever heard of, I anticipated much pleasure and advantage from his company and guidance through the western part of the peninsula. But my journey through Michigan is now nearly finished, as it began, entirely alone. At White Pigeon, where I found quite a pretty village of four years' growth, I seemed, in getting upon the post-route from Detroit to Chicago, to get back once more to an old country. I found a good inn and attendance at Savary's, and discovered, by the travellers going north and south, that travelling was not as yet completely frozen up. There are a great many English emigrants settled upon this prairie, who, I am told, are successfully introducing here the use of live hedges instead of fences in farming. They are generally of a respectable class, and seem to be quite popular with the American settlers.

The morning was fine when I left White Pigeon

to-day; and as the sun shot down through the tall woods, nothing could be more cheering than my ride among the beautiful hills of Cass county. The road, which is remarkably good, meanders through ravines for a distance of many miles, the conical hills resting upon the plain in such a manner as barely to leave a wheel-track between them, except when at times some pretty lake or broad meadow pushes its friths far within their embrace. A prairie of some extent was to be traversed on this side of these eminences, and the floating ice on the St. Joseph's was glistening beneath its shadowy banks in the rays of the cold winter moon when I reached its borders, and arrived at the stage-house in this flourishing town of Niles. Mine host, who does not seem to be the most accommodating person in the world, has refused to provide supper for myself and two other gentlemen at so late an hour, assigning as a reason that "his women are not made of steel,"—an instance of cause and effect which I merely put upon record as being the only one of the kind I have met with in all Michigan. My fellow-sufferers appear to be both agreeable men; and as we are to travel in company to Chicago, the sympathy arising from our present melancholy condition may ensure a pleasant intercourse under happier auspices.

The county of Cass, through which I have passed to-day, has a population of more than 2000, and contains seven prairies of six or eight miles in diameter, besides many smaller ones. They produce, when cultivated, from thirty to eighty bushels of new corn, of forty of wheat, to the acre. The mode of planting the former is to run a furrow, drop the corn in, and cover it with a succeeding furrow, which is planted in a similar way, and the field is rarely either ploughed or hoed after planting. There are several pretty lakes in this county; but it is not so well watered as St. Joseph's, through which I passed yesterday, which for local advantages of every kind, as well as fertility of soil, is generally considered one of the best in the peninsula. I like Kalamazoo county, however, as much as any part of Michigan I have seen. I am now within eight or ten miles of the Indiana boundary, and some twenty or thirty only from the shores of Lake Michigan, having described nearly a semicircle in my tour through the peninsula, including, with some deviations, the counties of Wayne, Monroe, Lenawee, and Washtenaw on the east, Jackson in the centre, and Calhoun, Kalamazoo, St. Joseph's, Cass, and Berrien on the west; and I have not met a resident in that whole range but what was pleased with the country, and I may almost say attached to its soil. The females indeed will sometimes murmur; and in some remote places I have heard those whose conversations indicated that they had not been brought up with the most ordinary advantages, complain of "the want of society!" But even these would love to dilate upon the beauties of the country when the flowers were in bloom. Others again, who had been more gently nurtured, would sigh at one moment for the comforts and elegancies of their maternal homes, while their eyes would kindle with enthusiasm the next, when speaking of the appearance which the woods around their new dwellings wore in summer. Small communities form but slowly in a country where the settlers, instead of gradually pushing their way together into the depths of the forest, as at the Eastward, drive their wagons in any direction a hundred miles through the openings, and plant themselves down a day's journey apart, just where their fancy prompts them. This will account for my so often lighting upon a pleasant hamlet, after a day's travel through a perfect wilderness.

The river St. Joseph debouches into Lake Michigan in this county; and as a steamboat will probably run the next season from the town rapidly growing at its mouth to Chicago, a rail-road from Detroit to this steamboat-harbour is only wanting to bring the visiter of Niagara within a few days' travel of Chicago, and carry him through the flowery groves of Michigan to one of the most important points in the Union, and what may be termed the central head of the Mississippi Valley. Delmonico may then stock his larder with grouse from the meadows of Michigan, and Gassin try his skill upon the delicious fish that swarm her lakes and rivers (would that I could at this moment witness some of their curious orgies) ; while sportsmen will think no more of a trip hither than they do now of an excursion to Islip, Rayner-South, or Patchogue. In the mean time I have secured you the seeds of more than twenty varie-ties of wild flowers, which I shall send to their destination as soon as possible, lest, from the rapid increase of internal communication, they may lose half their value from ceasing to be a rarity.

LETTER XVII.

Door Prairie, Indiana, Dec. 29, 1833.

Being now on the mail route between Detroit and Chicago, I am travelling very comfortably in a four-horse wagon, with the gentlemen mentioned in my last. I found my horse's back so chafed at White Pigeon, that it was unpleasant to use him longer under the saddle; and having met with my trunk at Niles, which was forwarded from Monroe by a friend, I am in a measure compelled to adopt what is certainly the most agreeable mode of travelling at this season through a bleak prairie country.

The cold winter moon was still riding high in the heavens as we ferried over the St. Joseph's at Niles this morning. A low-sided scow was the means of conveyance; and after breaking the solid ice near the shore to loose us from our moorings, it required some pains to shun the detached cakes which came driving down the centre of the dark rolling river; while, near the opposite shore, they had become so wedged and frozen together that it required considerable exertion to break a way with our long poles, and make good our landing. At length, ascending the bank, a beautiful plain, with a clump of trees here and there upon its surface, opened to our view. The establishment of the Carey Mission,* a long, low white building, could be distinguished afar off faintly in the moonlight, while several winter† lodges of the Pottawattamies, three or four hundred of which tribe inhabit this fine district, were plainly perceptible over the plain. The moon, indeed, shone with an effulgence such as I have never witnessed, except beneath the pearly skies of the west. Morning came at last; still, but excessively cold, our horses' manes and our own clothes being covered with hoar-frost, while each blade of grass that shot its wilted spear above the snow glistened like a diamond's point beneath the uprising sun.

About ten o'clock we reached a shanty on Terre Coupé prairie, and finding no one at home, we rummaged the establishment to find the materials for a breakfast, which we cooked ourselves, and left payment upon the table. Our next stage carried us over a *rolling prairie* to Laporte. The undulating surface resembled the ground-swell of the sea; and nothing could be more dreary, at this season, when

---

* See note H.   † See note I.

the bright sky of the morning became overcast, than moving mile after mile over this frozen lake— for such it appeared—with nothing but its monotonous swell to catch the eye wherever its glances roamed.

It was afternoon when we reached the little settlement of Laporte, which is situated on a pretty lake, in a prairie of the same name, the skirts of which are beautifully timbered. There was just light enough remaining when we reached our present stopping-place, a comfortable log-cabin, to see the opening ahead through the timber, from which this prairie takes its name. It forms a door opening upon an arm of the Grand Prairie, which runs through the States of Indiana and Illinois, and extends afterward, if I mistake not, to the base of the Rocky Mountains. I am now in the land of the *Hooshiers*, and find that long-haired race much more civilized than some of their western neighbours are willing to represent them. The term "Hooshier," like that of Yankee, or Buck-eye, first applied contemptuously, has now become a *soubriquet* that bears nothing invidious with it to the ear of an Indianian. This part of the State is as yet but thinly settled, but the land is rapidly coming into market, and it is calculated to support a dense population. A new town and harbour, called "Michigan City," about thirty miles off, on the shore of the lake, is fast coming into notice, and giving a spur to the settlements in these parts. The country is, however, still wild enough, and I have a wilder yet to pass, before reaching Chicago.

Chicago, Jan. 1, 1834.

We left the prairie on the east, after passing through "the door," and entered a forest, where the enormous black-walnut and sycamore trees cumbered the soil with trunks from which a comfortable dwelling might be excavated. The road was about as bad as could be imagined ; and after riding so long over prairies as smooth as a turnpike, the stumps and fallen trees over which we were compelled to drive, with the deep mud-holes into which our horses continually plunged, were any thing but agreeable. Still, the stupendous vegetation of the forest interested me sufficiently to make the time, otherwise enlivened by good company, pass with sufficient fleetness, though we made hardly more than two miles an hour throughout the stage. At last, after passing several untenanted sugar-camps* of the Indians, we reached a cabin prettily situated on the banks of a lively

* See note J.

brook, winding through the forest. A little Frenchman waited at the door to receive our horses,
while a couple of half-intoxicated Indians followed
us into the house, in the hope of getting *a'netos*
(vulgarly, "a treat") from the new comers. The
usual settlers' dinner of fried bacon, venison cutlets,
hot cakes and wild honey, with some tolerable tea
and Indian sugar, as that made from the maple-
tree is called at the West, was soon placed before
us; while our new driver, the frizzy little Frenchman already mentioned, harnessed a fresh team,
and hurried us into the wagon as soon as possible.
The poor little fellow had thirty miles to drive
before dark, on the most difficult part of the route
of the line between Detroit and Chicago. It was
easy to see that he knew nothing of driving, the
moment he took his reins in hand; but when one
of my fellow-travellers mentioned that little *Victor*
had been preferred to his present situation of trust
from the indefatigable manner in which, before the
stage route was established last season, he had for
years carried the mail through this lonely country
—swimming rivers and sleeping in the woods at
all seasons,—it was impossible to dash the mixture
of boyish glee and official pomposity with which
he entered upon his duties, by suggesting any improvement as to the mode of performing them.

Away then we went, helter skelter, through the
woods—scrambled through a brook, and galloping
over an arm of the prairie, struck again into the
forest. A fine stream, called the Calaminc, made
our progress here more gentle for a moment. But
immediately on the other side of the river was an
Indian trading-post, and our little French Phaeton
who, to tell the truth, had been repressing his fire
for the last half-hour, while winding among the
decayed trees and broken branches of the forest,
could contain no longer. He shook the reins on
his wheel-horses, and cracked up his leaders, with
an air that would have distinguished him on the
Third Avenue, and been envied at Cato's. He
rises in his seat as he passes the trading-house; he
sweeps by like a whirlwind: but a female peeps
from the portal, and it is all over with poor
Victor.

> " Ah, wherefore did he turn to look?
> That pause, that fatal gaze he took,
> Hath doomed—"

his discomfiture. The infuriate car strikes a
stump, and the unlucky youth shoots off at a tan-
gent, as if he were discharged from a mortar.
The whole operation was completed with such
velocity, that the first intimation I had of what

was going forward was on finding myself two or three yards from the shattered wagon, with a tall Indian in a wolf-skin cap standing over me. My two fellow-passengers were dislodged from their seats with the same want of ceremony; but though the *disjecta membra* of our company were thus prodigally scattered about, none of us providentially received injury. Poor Victor was terribly crest-fallen; and had he not unpacked his soul by calling upon all the saints in the calendar, in a manner more familiar than respectful, I verily believe that his tight little person would have exploded like a torpedo. A very respectable-looking Indian female, the wife, probably, of the French gentleman who owned the post, came out, and civilly furnished us with basins and towels to clean our hands and faces, which were sorely bespattered with mud, while the gray old Indian before mentioned assisted in collecting our scattered baggage.

The spot where our disaster occurred was a sequestered, wild-looking place. The trading establishment consisted of six or eight log-cabins of a most primitive construction, all of them gray with age, and so grouped on the bank of the river as to present an appearance quite picturesque. There was not much time, however, to be spent in observing its beauties.   The sun was low, and we had twenty-five miles yet to travel that night before reaching the only shanty on the lake-shore. My companions were compelled to mount two of the stage-horses, while I once more put the saddle on mine ; and leaving our trunks to follow a week hence, we slung our saddle-bags across the cruppers, and pushed directly ahead.

A few miles' easy riding through the woods brought us to a dangerous morass, where we were compelled to dismount and drive our horses across, one of the party going in advance to catch them on the other side.   A mile or two of pine barrens now lay between us and the shore, and winding rapidly among the short hills covered with this stinted growth, we came suddenly upon a mound of white sand at least fifty feet high.   Another of these desolate-looking eminences, still higher, lay beyond.   We topped it ; and there, far away before us, lay the broad bosom of Lake Michigan, —the red disk of the sun just sinking beneath it, and the freshening night-breeze beginning to curl its limpid waters on the shore ; and now, having gained their verge, whichever way we turned, there was nothing discernible but the blackening lake on one side and these conical hills of shifting white sand on the other.   Some of them, as the night advanced, and objects were only discernible by the bright starlight, assumed a most fantastic appearance, and made me regret that I could not visit the "Sleeping Bear," and other singularly-formed mounds, which, many miles farther to the north, swell from two to three hundred feet above the level of the lake.   The deep sand, into which our horses sunk to the fetlocks, was at first most wearisome to the poor beasts; and having twenty miles yet to travel entirely on the lake-shore, we were compelled, in spite of the danger of quick-sands, to move as near the water as possible.   But though the day had been mild, the night rapidly became so cold that, before we had proceeded thus many miles, the beach twenty yards from the surf was nearly as hard as stone, and the finest Mac-adamized road in the world could not compare with the one over which we now galloped.   Nor did we want lamps to guide us on our way. Above, the stars stood out like points of light, while the resplendent fires of the Aurora Borealis, shooting along the heavens on our right, were mocked by the livid glare of the Kankakee marshes burning behind the sand-hills on our left.   The lake alone looked dark and lowering; though even its gathering waves would smile when touched with light as they broke upon the shore.   The intense cold seemed to invigorate our horses; and dashing the fire from the occasional pebbles, they clattered along the frozen beach at a rate that brought us rapidly to our destination for the night.

It was a rude cabin, built of stems of the scrub pine, standing behind a sandy swell about two hundred yards from the shore. My fingers were numb with cold; and seeing a rough-looking fellow moving from the door towards the horses of my companions, I requested him to take mine also; but upon his politely rejoining that "he was nobody's servant but his own," I could only wish him "a more civil master;" and proceeded to take care of the animal myself. A brake of stunted evergreens, near-by, supplied the place of a stable; and passing a whisp of dry grass over the reeking limbs of my four-footed friend, I flung my cloak over his back and tethered him for the night. The keeper of the rustic hostelrie came up just as I had got through with this necessary task, and explaining to me that the insolent lounger was a discharged mail-carrier, returned with me to the house for a measure of corn; while I, guided by the light flickering through the crevices of his frail dwelling, rejoined my companions, nestled with two other half-frozen travellers around the grateful fire within.   The strangers were both western men ; one, I believe, a farmer, for some time settled in Illinois, and the other an Indian trader of long standing in Chicago.   Warlike incidents in border story, and the pacific dealings between the whites and Indians, formed the chief subjects of conversation, which soon became general, and was prolonged to a late hour ; finally, the late treaty held at Chicago—at which, as you have probably seen in the newspapers, several thousand Indians were present—was discussed, and the anecdotes that were told of meanness, rapacity, and highway robbery (in cheating, stealing, and forcibly taking away) from the Indians exasperated me so that I expressed my indignation and disgust in unmeasured terms.   The worthy trader, who was a middle-aged man, of affable, quiet good manners, seemed to sympathize with me throughout ; but the whole current of my feelings was totally changed, when, upon my observing shortly afterward to another gentleman, that " I should have liked to have been at Chicago a year ago," my warm coadjutor ejaculated from under the bed-clothes where he had in the mean time bestowed himself, " Ah, sir, if you had, the way in which you'd have hooked an Indian blanket by this time would be curious."   The chivalric knight of

La Mancha himself could not have sustained
heroics under such a home-thrust, but must have
burst into the hearty laugh in which I was joined
by all present.   The hour of sleep for all at last
arrived, and a couple of wooden bunks, swung
from the roof, falling to the lot of those who had
come in first, I wrapped myself in a buffalo-skin,
and placing my saddle under my head for a pillow,
soon " slept like a king ;" a term which, if

> " Uneasy lies the head that wears a crown"

be true doctrine, is, probably, *quasi lucus*, &c.

Our transient acquaintances parted from us in a
most friendly manner in the morning ; and after
waiting in vain till near noon, to see if by any chance
little Victor might not be able to forward our
trunks to this point, we mounted once more, and
pushed ahead with all speed, to accomplish the remaining twenty or thirty miles between the shanty
and Chicago.   Our route was still along the shore ;
and after passing round the end of the lake and taking a northwardly direction, the way in which the icy
blast would come down the bleak shore of the lake
" was a caution."   We galloped at full speed,
every man choosing his own route along the
beach, our horses' hoofs ringing the while as if it
were a pavement of flint beneath them.   The rough

ice piled up on the coast prevented us from watering
our beasts; and we did not draw a rein till the
rushing current of the Calaminc, which debouches
into Lake Michigan some ten miles from Chicago,
stayed our course.   A cabin on the bank gave us a
moment's opportunity to warm, and then being ferried over the wintry stream, we started with fresh
vigour, and crossing about a mile of prairie in the
neighbourhood of Chicago, reached here in time for
an early dinner.   Our horses this morning seem
none the worse for this furious riding; their
escape from ill consequences being readily attribut-
able to the excellence of the road, and the extreme
coldness of the weather while travelling it.   For
my own part, I never felt better than after this violent burst of exercise.   We had not been here an
hour before an invitation to a public ball was
courteously sent to us by the managers; and
though my soiled and travel-worn riding-dress was
not exactly the thing to present one's self in before
ladies of an evening, yet, in my earnestness to see
life on the frontier, I easily allowed all objections to
be overruled by my companions, and we accordingly drove to the house in which the ball was given.
It was a frame-building, one of the few as yet to
be found in Chicago; which, although one of the
most ancient French trading-posts on the Lakes, can

only date its growth as a village since the Indian war, eighteen months since.* When I add that the population has *quintupled* last summer, and that but few mechanics have come in with the prodigious increase of residents, you can readily imagine that the influx of strangers far exceeds the means of accommodation ; while scarcely a house in the place, however comfortable looking outside, contains more than two or three finished rooms. In the present instance, we were ushered into a tolerably sized dancing-room, occupying the second story of the house, and having its unfinished walls so ingeniously covered with pine-branches and flags borrowed from the garrison, that, with the white-washed ceiling above, it presented a very complete and quite pretty appearance. It was not so warm, however, that the fires of cheerful hickory, which roared at either end, could have been readily dispensed with. An orchestra of unplaned boards was raised against the wall in the centre of the room ; the band consisting of a dandy negro with his violin, a fine military-looking bass drummer from the fort, and a volunteer citizen, who alternately played an accompaniment upon the flute and triangle. Blackee, who flourished

* See note K.

about with a great many airs and graces, was decidedly the king of the company, and it was amusing,
while his head followed the direction of his fiddle-
bow with pertinacious fidelity, to see the Captain
Manual-like precision with which the soldier dressed
to the front on one side, and the nonchalant air of
importance which the cit attempted to preserve on
the other. As for the company, it was such a
complete medley of all ranks, ages, professions,
trades, and occupations, brought together from all
parts of the world, and now for the first time brought
together, that it was amazing to witness the deco-
rum with which they commingled on this festive
occasion. The managers (among whom were some
officers of the garrison) must certainly be *au fait*
at dressing a lobster and mixing regent's punch, in
order to have produced a harmonious compound
from such a collection of contrarieties. The gayest
figure that was ever called by quadrille playing
Benoit never afforded me half the amusement that
did these Chicago cotillons. Here you might see
a veteran officer in full uniform balancing to a
tradesman's daughter still in her short frock and
trousers, while there the golden aiguillette of a
handsome surgeon flapped in unison with the glass
beads upon a scrawney neck of fifty. In one quarter, the high-placed buttons of a linsey-woolsey

coat would be *dos à dos* to the elegantly turned shoulders of a delicate-looking southern girl; and in another, a pair of Cinderella-like slippers would chassez cross with a brace of thick-soled broghans, in making which, one of the lost feet of the Colossus of Rhodes may have served for a last. Those raven locks, dressed *à la Madonne*, over eyes of jet, and touching a cheek where blood of a deeper hue, mingling with the less glowing current from European veins, tell of a lineage drawn from the original owners of the soil; while these golden tresses, floating away from eyes of heaven's own colour over a neck of alabaster, recall the Gothic ancestry of some of "England's born." How piquantly do these trim and beaded *leggins* peep from under that simple dress of black, as its tall nut-brown wearer moves, as if unconsciously, through the graceful mazes of the dance. How divertingly do those inflated gigots, rising like windsails from that little Dutch-built hull, jar against those tall plumes which impend over them like a commodore's pennant on the same vessel. But what boots all these incongruities, when a spirit of festive good-humour animates every one present. " It takes all kinds of people to make a world" (as I hear it judiciously observed this side the moun-

tains), and why should not all these kinds of people
be represented as well in a ball-room as in a legislature? At all events, if I wished to give an intelligent foreigner a favourable opinion of the manners
and deportment of my countrymen in the aggre-
gate, I should not wish a better opportunity, after
explaining to him the materials of which it was
composed, and the mode in which they were brought
together from every section of the Union, than was
afforded by this very ball. "This is a scene of
enchantment to me, sir," observed an officer to me,
recently exchanged to this post, and formerly sta-
tioned here. "There were but a few traders
around the fort when I last visited Chicago, and
now I can't contrive where the devil all these well-
dressed people have come from!" I referred him
to an old resident of three months' standing, to
whom I had just been introduced, but he could
throw no light upon the subject, and we left the
matter of peopling Chicago in the same place where
philosophers have put the question of the original
peopling of the Continent. I made several new
acquaintances at this New-year's ball, and particularly with the officers of the garrison, from whose
society I promise myself much pleasure during my
stay. The geographical position of Chicago is so

important that I must give you a more minute description of the place in my next.   Would that in folding this I could enclose you half the warm wishes for your welfare which the season awakens in my bosom.

LETTER XVIII.

Chicago, Illinois, Jan. 10, 1834.

I have been here more than ten days, without fulfilling the promise given in my last. It has been so cold, indeed, as almost to render writing impracticable in a place so comfortless. The houses were built with such rapidity, during the summer, as to be mere shells; and the thermometer having ranged as low as 28 below zero, during several days it has been almost impossible, notwithstanding the large fires kept up by an attentive landlord, to prevent the ink from freezing while using it, and one's fingers become so numb in a very few moments when thus exercised, that, after vainly trying to write in gloves, I have thrown by my pen, and joined the group, composed of all the household, around the bar-room fire. This room, which is an old log-cabin aside of the main house, is one of the most comfortable places in town, and is, of course, much frequented; business being, so far as one can judge from the concourse that throng it, nearly at a stand still. Several persons have been severely frost-bitten in passing from door to door; and not to mention the quantity of poultry and pigs that have been frozen, an ox, I am told, has perished from cold in the streets at noonday. An occasional Indian,* wrapped in his blanket, and dodging about from store to store after a dram of whiskey, or a muffled-up Frenchman, driving furiously in his cariole on the river, are almost the only human beings abroad; while the wolves, driven in by the deep snows which preceded this severe weather, troop through the town after nightfall, and may be heard howling continually in the midst of it.

The situation of Chicago, on the edge of the Grand Prairie, with the whole expanse of Lake Michigan before it, gives the freezing winds from the Rocky Mountains prodigious effect, and renders a degree of temperature which in sheltered situations is but little felt, almost painful here.

> " The bleak winds
> Do sorely ruffle ; for many a mile about,
> There's scarce a bush."

The town lies upon a dead level, along the banks of a narrow forked river, and is spread over a wide extent of surface to the shores of the lake, while vessels of considerable draught of water can, by

* See note L.

means of the river, unload in the centre of the place. I believe I have already mentioned that four-fifths of the population have come in since last spring: the erection of new buildings during the summer has been in the same proportion; and although a place of such mushroom growth can, of course, boast of but little solid improvement in the way of building, yet contracts have been made for the ensuing season which must soon give Chicago much of that metropolitan appearance it is destined so promptly to assume. As a place of business, its situation at the central head of the Mississippi Valley will make it the New-Orleans of the north; and its easy and close intercourse with the most flourishing eastern cities will give it the advantage, as its capital increases, of all their improvements in the mode of living.

There is one improvement to be made, however, in this section of the country, which will greatly influence the permanent value of property in Chicago. I allude to a canal from the head of Lake Michigan to the head of steam navigation on the Illinois, the route of which has been long since surveyed. The distance to be overcome is something like ninety miles; and when you remember that the head-waters of the Illinois rise within eleven

miles of Chicago River,* and that a level plain of
not more than eight feet elevation above the latter
is the only intervening obstacle, you can conceive
how easy it would be to drain Lake Michigan into
the Mississippi by this route; boats of eighteen
tons having actually passed over the intervening
prairie at high water. Lake Michigan, which is
several feet or more above Lake Erie, would afford
such a never-failing body of water that it would
keep steamboats afloat on the route in the driest
season. St. Louis would then be brought comparatively near to New-York, while two-thirds of
the Mississippi Valley would be supplied by this
route immediately from the markets of the latter.
This canal is the only remaining link wanting to
complete the most stupendous chain of inland communication in the world. I had a long conversation this morning, on the subject, with Major H.,
the United States' engineer, who is engaged in
superintending the construction of a pier at this
place. He was polite enough to sketch the main
features of the route with his pencil, in such a
manner as to make its feasibility very apparent.
The canal would pass for the whole distance
through a prairie country, where every production
of the field and the garden can be raised with

* See note M.

x 2

scarcely any toil, and where the most prolific soil in the world requires no other preparation for planting than passing the plough over its bosom. The most effectual mode of making this canal would be to give the lands along its banks to an incorporated company, who should construct the work within a certain time. The matter is now merely agitated at elections as a political handle.

January 13.

I had got thus far in a letter to you, when several officers of the garrison, to whom I am indebted for much hospitable attention and many agreeable hours, stopped opposite the door with a train of carioles, in one of which I was offered a seat, to witness a pacing-match on the ice. There were several ladies with gentlemen in attendance already on the river, all muffled up, after the Canadian fashion, in fur robes, whose gay trimmings presented a rich as well as most comfortable appearance. The horses, from which the most sport was expected, were a black pony bred in the country, and a tall roan nag from the lower Mississippi. They paced at the rate of a mile in something less than three minutes. I rode behind the winning horse one heat, and the velocity with which he made our cariole fly over the smooth ice was almost startling. The southern horse won the race; but I was told that in nine cases out of ten, the nags from his part of the country could not stand against a French pony.

In the middle of the chase, a wolf, probably roused by the sleigh-bells from his lair on the river's bank, trotted along the prairie above, within gun-shot, calmly surveying the sport. The uninvited presence of this long-haired amateur at once suggested a hunt for the morrow, and arrangements were accordingly made, by the several gentlemen present, for that most exciting of sports, a wolf-chase on horseback.

I was not present at the assembling of the hunt; and the first intimation I had of the game being afoot, was from hearing the cry of hounds and the shouting of a party of horsemen, as they clattered along the frozen river, with two prairie wolves and one gray wolf running at full speed, about a pistol-shot ahead of them. One wolf was killed, and another had made his escape, before I joined the party. But the third, the gray wolf, which had struck off into the prairie, was still fresh when I came into the hunt with an untired horse. But one of the hunters had been able to keep up with him, and him I could distinguish a mile off in the prairie, turning and winding his foaming horse as the wolf would double every moment upon his tracks, while half a dozen dogs, embarrassed in the deep snow, were slowly coming up. I reached the spot just as the wolf first stood at bay. His bristling back, glaring eyes, and ferociously distended jaws might have appalled the dogs for a moment, when an impetuous greyhound, who had been for some time pushing through the snow-drifts with unabated industry, having now attained a comparatively clear spot of ground, leaped with such force against the flank of the wolf as to upset him in an instant, while the greyhound shot far ahead of the quarry. He recovered himself instantly, but not before a fierce, powerful hound, whose thick neck and broad muzzle indicated a cross of the bull-dog blood with that of a nobler strain, had struck him first upon the haunch, and was now trying to grapple him by the throat. Down again he went, rolling over and over in the deep snow, while the *clicking* of his jaws, as he snapped eagerly at each member of the pack that by turns beset him, was distinctly audible. The powerful dog, already mentioned, secured him at last, by fixing his muzzle deeply into the breast of the prostrate animal. This, however, did not prevent the wolf giving some fearful wounds to the other dogs which beset him; and, accordingly, with the permission of the gentleman who had led the chase, I threw myself from my horse, and gave the game the coup de grace with a dirk-knife which I carried about me. The success of this hunt induced us, upon the spot, to appoint another for this day.

It was a fine bracing morning, with the sun shining cheerily through the still cold atmosphere far over the snow-covered prairie, when the party assembled in front of my lodgings, to the number of ten horsemen, all well mounted and eager for the sport. The hunt was divided into two squads; one of which was to follow the windings of the river on the ice, and the other to make a circuit on the prairie. A pack of dogs, consisting of a greyhound or two for running the game, with several of a heavier and fiercer breed for pulling it down, accompanied each party. I was attached to that which took the river; and it was a beautiful sight, as our friends trotted off in the prairie, to see their different coloured capotes and gayly equipped horses contrasted with the bright carpet of spotless white over which they rode, while the sound of their voices was soon lost to our ears, as we descended to the channel of the river, and their lessening figures were hid from our view by the low brush which in some places skirted its banks. The brisk trot in which we now broke, brought us rapidly to the place of meeting; where,

to the disappointment of each party, it was found
that neither had started any game. We now
spread ourselves into a broad line, about gunshot
apart from each other, and began thus advancing
into the prairie. We had not swept it thus more
than a mile, when a shout on the extreme left, with
the accelerated pace of the two furthermost riders
in that direction, told that they had roused a wolf.
" The devil take the hindermost," was now the
motto of the company, and each one spurred for
the spot with all eagerness. Unhappily, however,
the land along the bank of the river, on the right,
was so broken by ravines, choked up with snow,
that it was impossible for us, who were half a mile
from the game when started, to come up at all
with the two or three horsemen who led the pursuit. Our horses sunk to their cruppers in the
deep snow-drift. Some were repeatedly thrown ;
and one or two, breaking their saddle-girths, from
the desperate struggles their horses made in the
snow-banks, were compelled to abandon the chase
entirely. My stout roan carried me bravely
through all ; but when I emerged from the last
ravine on the open plain, the two horsemen who
led the chase, from some inequality in the surface
of the prairie, were not visible ; while the third, a
fleet rider, whose tall figure and Indian headdress

had hitherto guided me, had been just unhorsed, and abandoning the game afoot, was now wheeling off apparently with some other object in view. Following on the same course, we soon encountered a couple of officers in a train, who were just coming from a mission of charity in visiting the half-starved orphans of a poor woman, who was frozen to death on the prairie a day or two since— the wolves having already picked her bones before her fate became known. One by one, our whole party collected around to make inquiries about the poor children, and the two fortunate hunters soon after joined us, one of them with a large prairie wolf hanging to the saddle-bow.

It was now about eleven o'clock; we were only twelve miles from Chicago; and though we had kept up a pretty round pace, considering the depth of the snow, in coursing backward and forward since eight, our horses generally were yet in good condition, and we scattered once more over the prairie, with the hope of rousing more game.

Not ten minutes elapsed before a wolf, breaking from the dead weeds which, shooting eight or ten feet above the level of the snow, indicated the banks of a deep ravine, dashed off into the prairie pursued by a horseman on the right. He made instantly for the deep banks of the river, one of whose wind-

ings was within a few hundred yards. He had a
bold rider behind him, however, in the gentleman
who led the chase (a young educated half-blood,
of prepossessing manners, and well connected at
Chicago). The precipitous bank of the stream
did not retard this hunter for a moment, but dashing down to the bed of the river, he was hard upon
the wolf before he could ascend the elevation on the
opposite side. Four of us only reached the open
prairie beyond in time to take part in the chase.
Nothing could be more beautiful. There was not
an obstacle to oppose us in the open plain ; and all
our dogs having long since given out, nothing remained but to drive the wolf to death on horseback. Away, then, we went, shouting on his
track ; the hotly pursued beast gaining on us
whenever the crust of a deep snow-drift gave him
an advantage over the horse, and we in our turn
nearly riding over him when we came to ground
comparatively bare. The sagacious animal became at last aware that his course would soon be up
at this rate, and turning rapidly in his tracks as we
were scattered over the prairie, he passed through
our line and made at once again for the river. He
was cut off, and turned in a moment, by a horseman on the left, who happened to be a little behind
the rest ; and now came the keenest part of the

sport. The wolf would double every moment upon his tracks, while each horseman in succession would make a dash at, and turn him in a different direction. Twice I was near enough to strike him with a horse-whip, and once he was under my horse's feet; while so furiously did each rider push at him, that as we brushed by each other and confronted horse to horse, while riding from different quarters at full speed, it required one somewhat used " to turn and wind a fiery Pegasus" to maintain his seat at all. The rascal, who would now and then look over his shoulder, and gnash his teeth, seemed at last as if he was about to succumb—when, after running a few hundred yards in an oblique direction from the river, he suddenly veered his course, at a moment when every one thought his strength was spent; and gaining the bank before he could be turned, he disappeared in an instant. The rider nearest to his heels became entangled in the low boughs of a tree which grew near the spot; while I, who followed next, was thrown out sufficiently to give the wolf time to get out of view, by my horse bolting as he reached the sudden edge of the river. The rest of the hunt were consequently at fault when they came up to us; and after trying in vain to track our lost quarry over the smooth ice for half an hour, we were most vexatiously compelled to abandon the pursuit as fruitless, and return to the village with only one scalp as the reward of our morning's labour.

It was with no enviable feelings, I assure you, that, on making my arrangements, an hour ago, to start in the new line of stage-coaches which has just been established between this point and St. Louis, I found myself compelled to part with the friend to whom I was chiefly indebted for my share in the glorious sports I have just attempted to describe to you—the four-footed companion of my last six weeks' rambles. I remember being once struck with the remark of an ingenious writer, in the Library of Useful Knowledge, when, in discussing the real and the relative value of horses, he observes that the commonest hackney, if in every respect suiting his owner, is priceless to the possessor. A favourite horse, in fact, though his estimation may only depend upon the whim of his master, is one of this world's goods which can never be thoroughly replaced. It is not, however, when the charge of such property falls exclusively to grooms and others, from one end of the year to another, that you feel its value. The stall-fed palfry, which you drive along a turnpike from one hotel to another, and abandon when he falls sick for some other means of conveyance, with as little concern as you would exchange your trunk for a portmanteau, or vice versa, has but little hold on one's feelings in comparison with the hearty animal with which you wander away, where he meets with no care but such as you bestow upon him ; and when you in turn become wholly dependent upon him for over-coming distances and difficulties between places so remote from each other, that not only your comfort, but sometimes your personal safety, depend upon accomplishing the intervals within certain periods —when you push ahead through falling sleet, ford rivers, plunge through snow-banks, or cross morasses, where the matted grass, spreading its carpet over the shaking slough, embarrasses and wearies the step of your sagacious quadruped, while it prevents his feet from sinking into the dangerous quagmire beneath. Three weeks of such intercourse between man and brute are like three rainy days when one is shut up in a country-house with strangers. They cherish a fellowship more cordial than years of ordinary intercourse could engender. It is no little consolation to me that I leave my Bucephalus in excellent hands ; nor does this necessary separation so engross my sympathies that I have none to spare for other partings. Upon these, however, I shall not dilate here, though you must not be surprised to find me returning more than once hereafter to characters, scenes, and incidents at Chicago which I have hitherto left untouched.

LETTER XIX.

Banks of the Au Sable, Illinois, Jan. 15.

It was about eight o'clock, and a bright cold morning, when a handsome four-horse stage-coach, built in New-York, and placed with more liberality than judgment on a route where a broad-tired, low-hung, and light wagon would be much more appropriate,—drove up to my quarters at Chicago; and, having received my luggage, crossed the river on the ice, and was a few moments after travelling through the deep snow over the Grand Prairie. My fellow-passengers were, a respectable middle-aged female and a smartly dressed young man of amiable appearance, whose handsome broadcloth suit, worn as a travelling dress, bespoke the favoured beau of some country village, or possibly a thriving young clerk from the city, engaged upon some agency business, and travelling in the style which he thought would best comport with the dignity of his employers. The driver was also accompanied on the box by a well-made young half-blood Chippeway of about five-and-twenty, who had come down from Mackinaw to seek employment, and was now going farther south for the same object. The air being rather sharp on the prairie, the lady took her seat between the young gentleman and myself, and thus wedged in together, we contrived to keep very comfortable; though our near neighbourhood did not render us more communicative than people generally are after an early breakfast. We merely exchanged the ordinary commonplaces which custom exacts from people thus thrown together; and then, unless when a wolf passing near our track, or a particularly large pack of grouse rising before us, called forth some exclamation, but few words were spoken by any of the company. At length, after having counted six wolves within twice as many miles, we approached a grove of timber, where, while the trees grew quite densely in the centre, a few thin rows shot out like a reef of rocks from the shadowy island far into the prairie. Here, on the edge of a deep gully, through which winds the River Au Plaine, was the log-tavern at which the first stage of our day's journey, being twelve miles, concluded. The horses were in a complete foam with their exertions in getting through the deep snow-drifts across the prairie, and I easily persuaded the driver to abandon the comfortable but cumbersome vehicle which had brought us so far, and hitch his smoking team, which had still twelve miles to go, to a rough but strongly-built sled before the door. My fellow-passengers approved the arrangement, and subsequent events proved it a very fortunate one; for so deep was the snow on many parts of the road afterward traversed, that it would have been impracticable to get a wheel-carriage forward, and it must have been deserted on the prairie. There was much to do, however, about our new equipage, before we could get started; and while our driver looked after his horses, one of the passengers had to shovel the snow out of the sleigh, another to drive a pin through the tongue in order to fasten on the leaders; and a third, after filling the bottom with hay, to adjust the baggage, &c. &c. All this, with the aid of the stout Chippeway and the active young eastern traveller, was soon effected; and the former taking his seat with the driver on a board in front, while the latter shared half of my buffalo robes, and stowed himself upon the hay with me in the rear; *madame* was well accommodated, with the cushions taken from the stage, on a trunk placed in the middle; and some heated stones being brought from the house and placed beneath her feet just as we started, no grandmother could sit more comfortably in her cushioned pew in old

Trinity. A fast drive of twelve miles brought us
at noon to another island of timber, where a little
piquant girl of sixteen, with sloe-black eyes and
glossy locks as dark as night, arranged a plain but
neat meal for us, and gave a relish to the entertain-
ment by loosing one of the most vivacious tongues
I had heard wag in the last three months. Here
we changed horses, and a ride of sixteen miles
more brought us about nightfall to a place called
" Walker's Grave," where two or three log-huts
were sheltered from the north wind under an
island of tall timber, and in one of which we have
established ourselves for the night. A pile of bur-
oak, which makes a capital fire, flames up the
enormous wooden chimney before me, and a number of stout yeomen around it, engaged in discussing the price of horses on the Wabash, prevent me,
while handling a matter of such moment, from en-
larging more upon the few objects of interest
which have presented themselves to-day.

Ottawa, Illinois, January 16.

I was hardly dressed this morning, when my
only remaining fellow-traveller—the lady and the
half-blood having parted company last evening—
called me to the door to " see the cloud of *prairie
hens* before it." I looked out, and there indeed,

true enough, the oaks within gunshot of the porch were so loaded with grouse, that they showed more like a flock of pigeons than a covey of game birds. Having broken my gun, however, it was intolerably vexatious to see such capital shots thrown away, while these fine birds in those districts where I was prepared to bag them were too wild to approach within shooting distance at all. The sleigh soon after came to the door, our driver having diminished his team by two horses, to meet, probably, the reduction of passengers already mentioned; and about a hundred yards from the house we crossed a broad brook, known as the Au Sable River, and commenced ascending the bank beyond. But the snow was deep, and the heavy drift having had its surface frozen over during the preceding night, our single pair of horses were unable to drag through it the clumsy sled behind them. They plunged in up to their chests. "Go ahead, Sam! gie up, Major!" shouted the driver. But *Sam* was thoroughly planted; while the *Major*, in trying to sustain his military character by obeying orders, gave one spring, and, floundering over the traces, was buried in the snow up to his crupper, and placed, *nolens volens*, in full as quiescent a condition as the already settled Sam. For all of us to get out and take hold of the bits was the next

move ; but it wouldn't do. Sam, indeed, seemed
a little inclined to make a retrograde movement,
by kicking out the footboard with his heels ; while
the Major, having gathered new energy for another
charge, wasted his fire in lifting up his knees as
high as his mouth, and ineffectually throwing his
fore hoofs in advance on the crusted snow ; handling his feet the while much after the manner of
the rampant unicorn on a calico stamp, who, unmindful of the mottoed garter he treads under his
foot, so bravely paws the crown which the com-
plaisant lion is pushing towards him. The driver
at last became convinced of the necessity of returning for another pair of horses ; and a young
colt called Blackhawk, with a hoary old plough-
horse named Judge, were, after a little delay, procured, and placed in advance of Sam and the
Major on the top of the bank. Poor Sam seemed
to dislike having the Judge's fetlocks brought so
immediately in contact with his nose, they being
nearly on a horizontal line ; and he was accordingly inclined to retreat upon his haunches, beneath
which the snow formed so easy a cushion ; but a
single crack from the driver's whip sent the Major
charging so vigorously upon Blackhawk, that the
sable young chief gave a bound which carried us
through the difficulty in a trice, and sent our vehi-

cle skimming far over the prairie. The grove
in which we had passed the night soon vanished
from sight, and a boundless expanse of snow-
covered surface lay like an ocean before us. The
arch of the clear blue sky seemed to spring at
once from the silvered earth, which shone under
the bright January sun with an intensity almost
painful to the eye. The blue vault above, and the
white plain below, were the only objects that met
its glances, as they roamed for miles around : yet
no one could complain of sameness in the tints of
a picture so vast, a scene so illimitable. The im-
mensity of the prospect seemed to exclude the idea
of monotony, and perfect solitude was only wanting in such a scene to make one feel its grandeur.
The lively rattle of my companion, however, whose
society, after travelling so long entirely alone, I
found no slight acquisition, prevented me from
realizing its full effect; and when, after riding for
about twelve miles, an island of timber hove in
sight, while the beautiful sky of the morning
clouded over, and the cold wind, which began to
set in from the west, indicated that the twelve
miles we had yet to travel before we should reach
the first house across this arm of the prairie would
be any thing but agreeable,—I was contented to
wrap myself as closely as possible in my buffalo

robe, and join him in a game of *prairie loo*. Lest you might search vainly in Hoyle for this pastime, I must inform you that the game consists merely in betting upon the number of wild animals seen by either party, towards the side of the vehicle on which he is riding, a wolf or deer counting ten, and a grouse one. The game is a hundred; and you may judge of the abundance of these animals from our getting through several games before dinner, —my companion looing me with eleven wolves. Some of these fellows would stand looking at us, within half-gunshot, as we rode by them; while the grouse would rise continually from under our very horses' feet.

Before we had got through the twenty-four miles, the scene enacted at starting was to be repeated with improvement; for on coming to the edge of a frozen gully, our two leaders, in their anxiety to avoid former difficulties, gave such a spring that they sunk through the ice to their shoulders, on the opposite side; while the wheel-horses, being thrown down, were driven by the runners of the sleigh against the sharp edges of the ice thus exposed, and one of them was terribly lacerated. It was the unfortunate Sam, who, poor fellow, not having been watered since the morning, lay quietly on his side in the traces, with his fore-

legs up the slope, and his hinder ones in the pool,
eating the snow thus brought in contact with his
mouth, apparently perfectly unconscious of his
wounds.   Blackhawk and the Judge, of course,
came to an anchor when they found such an accu-
mulated weight dragging behind them; while the
spirited Major seemed to be thoroughly dejected
at this second discomfiture, and allowed us to turn
him over and put him on his feet with scarcely
the interposition of a struggle.   Not far from the
scene of this catastrophe we crossed the Au Page,
a narrow stream, with smooth banks, utterly di-
vested of shrubbery; and after, in the next eight
miles, encountering two or three tremendous snow-
banks, where our horses were frequently immersed
to their cruppers, and whence nothing but the
leaders, from their firm footing beyond, dragging
the wheel-horses through the heavy drift, could
have extricated us, we reached a beautiful grove
of elms and oaks, and stopped to change our worn-
out team.

Entering a log-cabin, not at all differing from
the usual dwellings of the frontier settlers, I found
a choice collection of books in one corner,—a volume, a fine old edition, of Algernon Sidney's works
being the first book I took up; and upon entering
into conversation with the occupants of the cabin,

I found that degree of general cultivation which, though not unfrequently met with on the frontier, still always strikes a stranger with novelty; and yet, I know no reason why the fullest expanding of the intellect is incompatible with the handling of an axe, or the most luxuriant development of the imagination with following the plough. The farmer, of all operatives, has, perhaps, the most time for improvement; and when he dwells in a land where, while Nature showers her choicest bounties, man passes towards it from every side, and contributes on his new coming to the general stock of ideas, keeping, by this lively interchange, those already afloat in active circulation, there is every thing in his circumstances to make him acute and reflective, and to liberalize his mind, if not to polish his manners.

It would be giving you a wrong impression, however, did I allow you to gather from this, that the oldest western settlers of this country are by any means so familiar with books as the emigrants from the east; for among the latter there are many persons of altered circumstances, who, having once enjoyed better opportunities for literary culture, carry the traces of their old habits with them into the new scenes to which they so readily adapt themselves. Fluency of language, with an ease and power of expression which sometimes swells to the dignity of eloquence, and often displays itself in terms of originality, at once humorous and forcible, constitute the conversational resources of the western man; but as his knowledge is gathered almost altogether from conversation, he wants that exact acquaintance with facts and things which enriches the intellectual armory of his eastern brother, in a similar situation of life. My opportunities as yet of forming an opinion might, perhaps, be questioned by one who did not know that the southern part of Michigan and the northern sections of Illinois are settled by people from almost every State in the Union. Having now traversed them both, I may venture the above observation, at least with you.

A dinner of grouse at this place came very opportunely after our keen ride of twenty-four miles over the prairie without once stopping; and, by way of varying our customary fare of bacon and corn-bread along the road, we purchased a few brace of these fine birds for a mere trifle, there being at hand a coopful of them just caught alive upon the premises.

It was just sunset when, after riding about thirteen miles over a dreary-looking prairie, we came suddenly to one of those *steppes* into which these singular plains sometimes break so beautifully; and, looking down over two broad platforms, which successively projected their flat surfaces and angular edges below us, beheld the Illinois River winding through the lowest meadow, and receiving its tributary, the Fox River, opposite the little village of Ottawa. It seemed to repose upon a rich alluvial flat, with the rocky bluffs of the Illinois rising in a regular line to the height of seventy or eighty feet immediately in the rear, while their rugged and varying outline, both above and below, towered opposite to a much greater height. The warm light of the setting sun resting upon their mossy edges, and touching with freshness an evergreen that sprouted here and there among the cliffs, while the rising mists of evening imparted a bluish tint to the distant windings of the smooth valley below, gave an Italian softness to the landscape, but little in unison with the icy rigours that enchained the streams to which in summer it must owe its greatest beauty. A mile or two farther brought us over the frozen river to the comfortable frame-house from which this letter is dated.

Ottawa, which is situated a few miles above the head of steamboat navigation on the Illinois, is, from its central situation, gradually becoming a place of some commercial importance, though still a mere hamlet in size. It was within six miles of this place that the worst of the Indian horrors were perpetrated during the difficulties with the Sacs and Foxes in 1832. You must remember the newspaper accounts of every member of two families being butchered, except two young girls, who were carried into captivity, and afterward recovered from the Indians.* There was a singular fatality attending this melancholy affair, which makes it worth while to recall some of the particulars. According to my informant, the heads of both families, who lived in the same or adjoining houses, had more than once removed their wives and children into Ottawa, upon false alarms of the approach of the Indians; and one of them, from some new warning on the very day on which the event took place, was again moving the united establishment in wagons to the same place of security, when he met the other, who so opposed and ridiculed the idea that they returned together. An hour or two after they were at work, within a few yards of the door, when a band of Indians appeared, and with a triumphant yell surrounded the house in an instant. Armed only with their tools of husbandry, they did not hesitate to make an at-

* See note N.

tack upon an enemy that outnumbered them so
as to make the attempt to get into the house and
reach their rifles perfect madness. It is needless
to add that they were shot down, tomahawked, and
scalped in an instant; not, however, as some say,
before they had witnessed some of the atrocities
practised upon the feebler members of their families.   These, both before and after death, are too
shocking to mention.

"Why, sir," said an Illinois man to me, who was
on the spot shortly afterward, "those Indians be-
haved most *ridiculous*. They dashed children's
brains against the door-posts; they cut off their
heads; they tore—;" but the detail to which my
informant applied so quaint an epithet is one that
I would not think for a moment of giving you.   I
must not forget to add, that the two surviving
females, after losing every near blood-relative in
this horrible manner, have lately found legal pro-
tectors, and are now settled in life as respectable
married women.   I had previously, even as far
north as the borders of Michigan in Indiana, seen
stockades erected in the open prairie as a place of
refuge for the settlers, with other similar marks of
the late border-strife, but had no idea till this evening that I was approaching the seat of the bloodiest
acts of the unhappy contest.   The neutral Indians,

who disappeared from this part of the country at the time, are now, I am told, dispersed again in large numbers over the neighbourhood.   They are perfectly harmless; but, though treated with great kindness by the new emigrants, there will probably never again be much confidence between them and the old settlers.   The latter somehow seem to have long regarded the Indians as hereditary enemies; and the events of 1832 have given new vigour to dislikes which seemed to be gradually losing their rancour.   A man who has to plough with a heavy rifle, ready-loaded, slung to his back, day after day, while he fears even to send his child to the spring for a pail of water, may be well excused for being warm upon a subject which must thus fill his thoughts and harass his mind throughout each hour of the day.   It is therefore useless to argue with an Illinois "Indian hater."   What cares he for the "lean famine, quartering steel, and climbing fire," which you tell him often beset the red man's wigwam before his ancestors made good their footing on another's land.   He thinks but of the frantic outrages he has witnessed in his own day.   He thinks of his often-abandoned husbandry, "while that the coulter rusts" corrupting in its own fertility.   He thinks of his butchered friends and neighbours,—of his wife and offspring slaughtered

upon his hearth-stone,—and asks bitterly how you
could

> " Look to see
>   The blind and bloody savage with foul hand
>   Defile the locks of your shrill-shrieking daughters ;
>   Your fathers taken by the silver beards,
>   And their most reverend heads dashed to the walls ;
>   Your naked infants spitted upon pikes,
>   While the mad mothers with their howls confused
>   Do break the clouds."

An accumulation of horrid images, which shows
with what fearful fidelity Shakspeare would have
painted Indian warfare, had these wild tragedies
of our day been acted in his.

LETTER XX.

Boyd's Grove, Illinois, Jan. 25th, 1834.

It was so long since I had seen a stone at all deserving the name of a rock, that I took a good deal of satisfaction in scaling the bluffs of the Illinois, and traversing the adjacent ravines, before getting out on the prairie the morning that I left Ottawa. In one of these rocky gullies,—which run generally at right angles to the river, and with their precipitous walls in one place, and cavernous passages beneath the jutting limestone in another, often form some picturesque dell, or afford a romantic glimpse of the open country beyond,—I saw the first cascade I have met with since leaving Pennsylvania. The fall was not more than ten feet ; but the column of water, being frozen in a solid sheet, as white as the purest porcelain, presented a very singular appearance as it raised its pale glistening front beneath a canopy of stunted cedars, whose green branches impended from the rocks above. Our sleigh, after winding for some time among this broken ground, and passing over one or two small but beautiful pieces of bottom land

lying among the ravines, reached at last the top
of the bluff, where, instead of descending on the
other side, the level prairie extended as far as the
eye could reach beyond. A few hours' drive
brought us to a log-cabin, which was our place for
dining and changing horses, and here we found
that, owing to the newness of the route, arrangements were not yet completed for the public conveyances going farther. Hearing a stranger speaking in terms of enthusiasm of the fine view from
" Starved Rock,"—a detached crag some 200 feet
high, on the banks of the Illinois, where one band of
Indians was surrounded and starved to death by
another (I refer you to " Flint's Valley of the Mis-
sisippi" for the legend),—I made arrangements to
visit the spot in the morning.

A chill north-easter swept over the bleak prairie
as my travelling companion and myself, mounted
upon two miserable nags, neither of which was
shod, struck on an Indian trail, that brought us in
an hour's ride to the craggy and precipitous banks
of the Vermilion River, which it was necessary to
cross. A sickly-looking but rather interesting
woman came out of a miserable log-hut—beside
which, housed under a few boards, stood a handsome barouche—to direct us where to descend the
bank ; and my friend on foot leading his horse,

mine followed trembling after him ; and, notwithstanding the steep path was glazed with ice, we descended the first pitch in safety.

Pausing for a moment, the confused masses of rock, with trees and shrubs of all kinds growing in their crevices, reminded me, as I looked around, of more than one scene of the kind in the river counties of my native State. It was now my turn to lead down the next pitch, which led to the frozen bed of the river. Upon gaining the edge I perceived that the descent was a perfect glare of ice ; and pausing a moment to hand a loaded gun, which I carried, to my companion, lest it might be discharged in the accident which I anticipated, my horse lost his footing even as I turned in the saddle, and falling flat over upon me, down we slid together. I had not gone two yards, however, before a small jutting rock brought me, but little bruised, to an anchorage, while my unfortunate consort, after sliding over a part of my person, went, though struggling fearfully to regain his feet, slipping to the bottom. He landed at last erect, with his face up the ascent, and though now on the level ice of the river, the poor brute seemed to think he was still midway on the declivity he had been hurried over so roughly ; for without looking at all behind him, he stood trembling for an instant, and then, in

spite of all the outcry we could raise to keep him
back, commenced ascending to where we stood,
and actually persevered till he had gained the
place from whence he had started.   The only way
now to effect our purpose was for one to go below,
and the other to drive the horses down to him.
This we indeed did, and I do not know when I
have been more amused, than upon seeing my
worthy Rozinante, as if taught by past expe-
rience, quietly—when he found he must go—
placing himself upon his haunches, and sliding
down the little hill with a degree of coolness and
skill that would have been envied by the boldest
schoolboy on *Flattenbarrack*.

Crossing the Vermilion, we were compelled to
drive our horses in the same way up the bank on
the opposite side; and by catching hold of the
branches of trees, drag ourselves after them as we
best could.   Once on the height, nothing but a level
plain of rich prairie land lay between us and the
bluffs of the Illinois.   It was crossed here and
there at intervals of a few miles with Indian trails,
about a foot in width, and worn as deep as if they
had been trod for centuries.   They ran in various
directions, and were generally as straight as the
flight of an arrow.   A heavy rain throughout the
previous night had swept all the snow from the

prairie, and these black lines drawn over its brown surface were now perceptible at a great distance. A long reach of woodland immediately before us indicated our approach to the Illinois bottoms; but on entering the timbered ground, where the snow still lingered in considerable quantities, we found ourselves on the slippery bluffs, a hundred feet above the level of the river opposite, without the possibility of descending to its bed. These bluffs were divided at intervals by the romantic ravines already described; and having now discovered that we had entirely missed the road to " The Starved Rock," it only remained for us to attempt descending through these passages, and find the place by a route of our own. We led the way by turns, and urging our unwilling horses down the frozen beds of the little streams which impart their coolness in autumn to these sequestered dells, we tried three ravines in succession, without attaining our object. One would bring us up against a dead wall of limestone, in the crevices of whose base the rill we had been following suddenly disappeared; a second carried us to the abrupt edge of a precipice, about fifty feet above the river, whose rich bottoms, extending far away below, reminded me, with the occasional copses and detached clumps of trees which studded them, of points of views in the valley of the Mohawk. Nothing, on so small a scale, could be more picturesque than the nook to which the third ravine led us. It was to the upper edge of a double cascade, over the second fall of which an arch of rock projected, so as to shut out from view the basin into which the water finally fell below. The passage through which we reached the spot was a mere fissure in the side-hill; and when, not wishing to get my feet wet, I urged my horse to the brink of the little cascade, the long icicles pendent from the hanging rock above were almost within reach of my riding-whip. A number of gnarled and stunted cedars, "moist trees, that have outlived the eagle," fling their dusky branches over the chasm, and when summer foliage glitters on the tall stems whose naked boughs project above them, the sun must be wholly excluded from this cool retreat.

Our horses were so fagged out when we extricated ourselves from this ravine, that we did not think it well to try another; and my companion being afraid of freezing his feet, which were wet from his having dismounted at the most difficult parts of the descent, I was sorry to be compelled to give up the search and return to our lodgings, after an eight hours' ride, without having seen the interesting point we had taken so much trouble to attain.*

The mail contractor, resident at Chicago, had arrived at the farm-house during our absence ; and hearing that two gentlemen were detained upon the road, had, with great politeness, at once taken measures to send us on the next morning. The room, too, in which we had slept before—four in two beds, and three on the floor—had now been

* An unknown correspondent has politely furnished the author with the following account of this interesting point, as given in " a letter from a friend, still roaming over the beautiful prairies of Illinois."

" I climbed the Indian path until I reached the summit of Starved Rock. This celebrated rock is said to be two hundred and fifty feet high. It is a stupendous pile, nearly as large at the top as at the base, and is accessible at one place only ; in every other direction it is nearly perpendicular, and more than half its base is washed by the Illinois, which is here from three to four feet deep.

" The summit is circular and almost level, containing about an acre ; and now has on it a thick growth of young timber. There is still lying a great quantity of the bones of the Indians who were starved to death by a hostile tribe. I picked up on the side of the pass, and dug out of the earth, several arrow-points. At one place, where there appears a possibility of scaling the rock, an intrench-ment is dug and breastwork thrown up. After passing an hour on the summit, we descended to our boat at the foot of the rock, and proceeded on our voyage."—See note O.

vacated by five of its occupants, and my companion
and I each appropriated a couch to himself. We
were hardly warm under the cover, however, before the tramping of horses, with the sound of
travellers' voices, was heard without; and the good
dame thrust her head into the room, in the vain expectation of showing them an unoccupied bed. My
companion pretended to be in a sound sleep; and I
intimated that I should betake myself to my buffalo
robe and the floor, in case a bed-fellow were thrust
in upon me : whereat the kind lady was exceedingly miffed; and we could hear her through the
board partition, a moment afterward, expressing
herself after this amiable fashion—" Ugh! great
people, truly!—a bed to themselves—the hogs!—
They travel together—and they eat together—and
they eat enough, too—and yet they can't sleep together!" Here the husband, a respectable middle-·
aged man, who did every thing to make our situation comfortable during the thirty-six hours we
spent at his cabin, interposed, and silenced his
better half; and the new comers, wrapping themselves in their cloaks before the fire, in a few
minutes all became still about the establishment.

The good dame, who must have been a fine-
looking woman in her day, and was, I believe, in
spite of her scolding ways, really well-disposed to-

wards us at heart, gave us a capital cup of coffee and a kind farewell in the morning. A four-horse wagon, with an active driver, quickly accomplished a mile of rough road through the grove, and brought us once more to the edge of the smooth prairie. I can conceive nothing more desolate than the appearance of that boundless plain. The fires had traversed it in the autumn as far as the eye could reach, and the snow having now disappeared entirely from the upland, the black and charred surface was all that met our vision wherever it wandered. A dark sullen sky which lowered overhead added not a little to the gloominess of the prospect; and the day being excessively cold, our ride for the next fifteen miles over this dreary plain was any thing but agreeable. At last we came to some broken ground, dotted here and there with a handful of shrubbery, from which every moment a pack of grouse and occasionally a bevy of quail would rise. The little village of Hennepin—called after Father Hennepin—next hove in sight; though it lay so sheltered along the banks of the Illinois that we were nearly upon the hamlet before its vicinity was discoverable.

After stopping an hour or two to dine and feed our horses, we left the driver to take a circuitous route down the steep bank, which, though not rocky, is about sixty feet high, and very precipitous on that side of the river, while my friend and I descended to the ice, and walked over the river, which was here a broad and noble stream, with some beautiful alluvial islands on its bosom. The difference of temperature here and on the bleak prairie above was astonishing; and when I sat down upon a fallen tree among the tangled vines of the rich bottom opposite to Hennepin, and watched a flock of green paroquets fluttering among the wych-elms which here and there skirted the shore, while the sun, for a moment piercing his murky veil, touched with gold the icicles that glazed their drooping branches, I could fancy myself transported to a different climate. The driver overtook us at last, and then we commenced making our way through a timbered bottom, which, for appearance of rank fertility, excelled any spot I have ever beheld. The trees, which were of enormous size, seemed chained together at every point by the huge vines which clambered to their very summits, locking the stately stems in their ponderous embrace, and clasping each outer bough with some twining tendril, which, having thus secured its prey on one tree, seemed like a living animal to have bounded to another, and fastened its eager grasp upon some limb as yet untouched. Beneath the whole an interminable growth of underwood, protected by the woven canopy above, and flourishing rankly in its living fetters,

> " Like prisoners wildly overgrown with hair,
>   Put forth disordered twigs."

A half-hour's ride carried us through this teeming region to the foot of a steep and open-wooded hill, which ascending with some difficulty, we came out once more upon the prairie, and found the change of temperature instantaneous. The road over the dry grassy plain was very good, however, for the first six or eight miles; and as the evening began to close in intensely cold, we rattled them off in a very short time. At last we came to a deep-frozen gully, in crossing which our leaders bruised themselves so badly by breaking through the ice, that when we reached a spot of the same kind, but rather worse, a mile or two in advance, the frightened animals recoiled from the place, and refused to cross it Our driver, a doughty little chap, about four feet eleven, who rejoiced in the name of Samson, and was a capital whip, by-the-by, after using every exertion to get his whole team over, was at last compelled to give up the point, and proceed to detach the leaders from the wheel-horses. This, with our aid, was soon done; and my companion remaining with the leaders on one side, Samson and I made a dash at the frozen brook, and, breaking through in the midst, the horses gave such a spring to free themselves from the wagon that the swingletree-bolt snapped; and had not the heroic little champion held on to the reins as tenaciously as did his namesake to the gates of Gaza, we might have been left a prey to the next drove of Philistinean wolves that should rove the prairie in quest of a supper. Samson, however, was true to his name; and with a mighty arm bringing up his foaming steeds all standing, we crawled over the head of the rampant wagon (the hind-wheels only had gone through the ice), and sprang to the firm ground. The swingletree was soon tinkered fast again; but now came the difficulty of getting the unwilling leaders over, who, it is presumed, had been no uninterested spectators of what had just been going forward; coaxing and whipping availed nothing; and we at last succeeded only by buckling two pair of reins together and passing them over the brook, two of us pulling on the horses' mouths, while the third applied a smart castigation behind. One of the poor animals again broke in, and floundered dreadfully before he reached a firm footing on the other side. But this was not the worst; our poor little

Samson, in attempting to jump, plunged in to his knees, and suffered much inconvenience from it afterward. The evening was indeed so cold that our wheel-horses, who were coated with ice, their long tails being actually frozen solid, were in danger of freezing to death, had we been compelled to delay much longer. But, placing now the leaders on the firm ground beyond them, one smart pull served to extricate the wagon from the hole, and deliver us from our quandary.

We had five or six miles still to go before reaching a house, and feeling some anxiety about Samson's wet feet, we urged him to put the horses—nothing loath when once started—to the top of their speed. He did indeed drive furiously; but when we arrived at the house whence I write, the poor fellow's feet were frozen. Rushing at once to the fire, he would undoubtedly have lost them, had there not chanced to be a physician present, who directed us what to do. The good-humoured little patient was removed without delay to the back part of the room; and we commenced pouring water into his boots until they melted from his feet, the temperature of the water being gradually heightened till it became blood-warm, while a bucket of ice-water stood by for the sufferer to thrust his feet in, whenever the returning circulation became too violent for him to endure.   In the morning, though his feet were dreadfully swollen, he was enabled, by tying them up in thick horse-blankets, to move about, and even return with his team.   To the simple and judicious suggestions of the travelling-physician present our little hero was, in all probability, indebted for escaping a most awful calamity:—a settler in this neighbourhood having lost both legs a few days since by an exposure similar to Samson's.

I am now staying at the house of a flourishing farmer, whose sturdy frame, bold features, and thick long black hair would, with his frank address, afford as fine a specimen of the western borderer as one could meet with, and never allow you to suspect that ten or fifteen years ago he was a New-York tradesman.   He lives, like all other people of this country, in a log-cabin, which has many comforts about it, however, not usually found in these primitive domicils.   Having a large family, with no neighbours nearer than ten miles on one side, and twenty on the other, he maintains a school-master to instruct his children: the room I occupy at night being fitted up with desks and benches as a school-room.   His farm, which lies along the edge, of a beautiful and well-watered grove, supplies him with almost every thing that he wants;

and having once pursued a different mode of life, he seems now to realize the full independence of his situation, more even than those who have always been brought up as farmers. I told him this morning, as he sallied out to chop, with his two sons, axe in hand, all clad in their belted capotes and white woollen hoods, that I should like to meet his sun-burnt features and independent step in Broadway, to see how many of his old acquaintances would recognise the pale mechanic in the brown back-woodsman. He promised me, if he came in winter, to appear with the guise in which I then beheld him, adding, in western phraseology, " The way in which folks 'll stare, squire, will be a *caution.*"

After being detained here some days, waiting for the St. Louis mail-wagon, and losing my travelling-companion, who, having bought a horse, has gone on by himself, I have concluded that it would never do to go out of this country without visiting Galena and the mining country: and as there is now a public conveyance thither, I shall take the first opportunity to go with it. I have amused myself for the last three nights in watching for wolves by moonlight, at the edge of the wood, a few hundred yards from the house. They come howling round the house after nightfall, and if on is " in luck" at all, are easily shot.   But last night, after leaving my position but for five minutes, I heard the report of a rifle, and hastening to the spot, where a lad staid to fill my place for a moment, I found that a gray and a black wolf, of the largest kind, had approached suddenly within two or three yards of the muzzle of his gun, and startled him so that he missed them both.   In the confident hope of their return—for the bait that we had thrown about the place was still there—I took the little fellow's place, and wrapping myself in a buffalo skin, lay watching on the ground till nearly daybreak ; and the enemy then not making his appearance, I was glad to creep shivering to bed.

Upon entering my room, which contained two beds, I observed, after striking a light, that the one opposite to mine was occupied by some newcomers, while a sheet suspended from the ceiling near the pillow, and concealing the phrenology of its occupants from view, was evidently meant as a *caveat* against reconnoitring that part of the apartment.   A respectable-looking traveller and a pretty young woman, who I was told was a bride on her way to St. Louis, breakfasted with us the next morning.   But, alas ! it completely destroyed the piquancy of my reflections, to see madam, after wrapping herself in a handsome cashmere shawl, while their sleigh was getting ready, raise her white lace veil, and place the stump of a *pipe* between her rosy lips! Can you conceive a more legitimate cause for divorce? "*An American bride smoking a pipe!*" What a subject for Cruickshank to illustrate, by way of frontispiece to the next edition of Captain Hamilton's "Men and Manners!"

You shall hear from me next at Galena. Till then, farewell.

LETTER XXI.

Galena, Upper Mississippi, Feb. 1.

A furious squall of snow, which would have rendered it impossible to keep a given road in crossing the prairie, subsided before night-fall, on the day that I left Boyd's Grove, bound for the Upper Mississippi; and as the calm clear sky of evening succeeded, our sleigh glided over the open plain at a rate which soon made the cabins behind us disappear in the distance; while four fleet horses, with a good driver, and but one passenger, swiftly accomplished the short stage of twelve miles, and brought us to the room where we were to pass the night. The intervening prairie, for the first six miles, was high and level, with not a stick of timber,—one broad snow-covered plain, where you could see the dark figure of a wolf for miles off, as it stood in relief against the white unbroken surface. A prospect more bleak and lonely, when night is closing in, and you press towards some distant grove, whose tree-tops cannot yet be discovered above the monotonous plains, is inconceivable. Presently, however, you come to a break in the prairie; a slight descent next shelters you somewhat from the wind, and now you can discover a wood, which hitherto had appeared many miles off, or perhaps was not perceptible at all, that has pushed a scattered clump of trees here and there, like an advanced guard under cover of the ravine. You come to the brink of another platform, and you are on the edge of a grove; while for twenty miles ahead the eye ranges over what looks like a shallow basin of immense extent, broken occasionally by dusky masses, which seem rather to repose upon than to spring out of its surface; such was the view in advance, from a point about six miles from Boyd's Grove. The elevation from which we descended was not more than twenty feet, and it commanded a prospect of as many miles. It was like looking from the edge of a snow-covered desert upon a frozen lake, with its isles, headlands, and scattered rocks, and its waters riveted as fast as they. The rosy rays of the setting sun still lingered over the scene, as on one they longed to set free from the icy chains which bound it; while the calm pale moon grew momentarily more bright, as if her cold beams borrowed lustre from the extent of pure white surface over which they shone.

A single room, miserably built of logs,—the interstices of which were so unskilfully filled up with mud that I could hear the night-wind whistling through them as we drove up to the door,— was to be our lodging for the night. A couple of rifles, with a powder-horn and a pair of Indian blankets, lay without, and two painted Pottawattamies were crouched on the hearth, as I entered the cabin. One of them, a slight but elegantly-formed youth of twenty, sprang at once to his feet ; while the other, a dark ill-looking negro-faced fellow, retained his squatting posture. They were dressed in complete suits of buckskin ; both having their ears bored in several places, with long drops of silver pendent in thick bunches therefrom ; while broad plates suspended over their chests, with armlets of the same metal, made quite a rich display. Their dress* was, however, the only point in which they resembled each other ; and the acquiline nose, keen eyes, and beautifully-arched brows of the one contrasted as strongly with the heavy inexpressive look and thick lips of the other, as did the closely-fitting hunting-frock of the first, which a black belt, sown thick with studs of brass, secured to his erect form, with the loose

* See note P.

shirt that crumpled around the crouching person
of the other. A hard-featured borderer, with
long sandy hair flowing from under a cap of wolf-
skin, and dressed in a bright green capote with an
orange-coloured sash, sat smoking a pipe on the
other side of the fireplace; while one foot dangled
from the bed on which he had placed himself, and
another rested on a Spanish saddle, whose holsters
were brought so near to the fire, as it lay thus care-
lessly thrown in a corner, that the brazen butts of
a pair of heavy pistols were continually exposed
to view by the flickering light. A pale, sickly-
looking woman, with an infant in her arms, and
two small children clinging around her lap, sat in
the centre, and completed the group. Her husband and another, a hanger-on of the establishment,
had stepped out to look after our horses, as we
drove up to the door. The apartment, which was
not more than twenty feet square, was cumbered
up with four beds; and when I thought how many
there were to occupy them, and observed a thin
cotton curtain flapping against a wide unglazed
opening, which formed the only window of this
forlorn chamber, I thought that the prospect of
comfortable accommodation for the night was any
thing but promising. Presently, however, the
landlord entered, with an armful of burr-oak and

split hickory, which crackled and sputtered at a rate that made the Indians withdraw from the ashes. The good woman placed her child in a rude cradle, and bestirred herself with activity and good-humour in getting supper; while the frontiers-man, knocking the ashes from his tomahawk-pipe, passed me a flask of Ohio whiskey, which, after my cold ride, had all the virtue of Monongahela. Some coarse fried pork, with a bowl of stewed hominy, hot rolls, and wild honey, did not then come amiss, especially when backed by a cup of capital coffee from the lower country; though the right good-will with which we all bent to this important business of eating did not prevent me from noticing the Frenchman-like particularity with which the Indians ate from but one dish at a time, though tasting every thing upon the table.

The best-looking of the two, though daubed with paint to a degree that made him look perfectly savage, was almost the only Indian I had yet found who could talk English at all; and he seemed both amused and interested while I read over to him a slight vocabulary of words in his own language, as I had taken down the terms occasionally in my pocket-book, and was evidently gratified when I added to their number from his lips. He spoke the language, indeed, with a clearness and distinctness of enunciation such as I have only heard before from a female tongue; and the words thus pronounced had a delicacy and music in their sound entirely wanting in the usual slovenly utterance of Indians. You would have been struck, too, in the midst of our philological task, to see the grim-looking savage bend over and rock the cradle, as the shivering infant would commence crying behind us. In this way the evening passed rapidly enough; and then the good dame with her husband and children taking one bed, the green rider and I took each another, while the stage-driver and remaining white man shared the fourth together. The Indians brought in their guns and blankets from without, and making a mattress of my buffalo-skin, they placed their feet to the fire, and after a chirping conversation of a few minutes beneath their woollen toggery, sunk to slumber.

The moon was still shining brightly above, as I sallied out an hour before dawn to wash in the snow, and finish in the open air the toilet commenced in the crowded shantee. Our sleigh, a low clumsy pine box on a pair of ox-runners, was soon after at the door, and covering up my extremities as well as I could in the wild-hay which filled the bottom (for the morning was intensely cold), I wound my fur robe around my head to keep my face from freezing, and soon found myself gliding at a prodigious rate over the smooth prairie. The sun was several hours high when we struck a fine grove of timber, through which the small but rapid river Huron takes its way, and thrashing through the wintry stream, we merely paused long enough at a shantee on the opposite side to adjust some of our harness which was broken while fording the torrent, and reached a comfortable log-cabin, in which we breakfasted at noon. There was an Indian encampment within gun-shot of the house, and seeing a melancholy-looking squaw with an infant in her arms, hanging about the farm-house, I left my landlady turning some venison cutlets and grilled grouse, to see how the aborigines fared in this cold weather. A pretty Indian girl of fourteen, driving a couple of half-starved ponies, indicated the camp of her friends. They proved to be a very inferior band, having but two hunters, and those inefficient-looking fellows, to a score of women and children. Sheer necessity had compelled them to encamp near the settlement; and a more squalid, miserable-looking set of creatures I never beheld. The chief of the party, contrary to the usual Indian custom, had let his beard* grow till it stood out in small tufts from every part of his sinister-looking smoke-dried face; and the thong of leather which sustained his scalping-knife seemed to answer the double purpose of binding the fragments of his greasy and tattered capote to his body, and of keeping the loosely hung component parts of the body itself together. A bluff-faced English-looking white youth of eighteen, with a shock head of reddish curly hair, and wearing a hunting-frock of some coarse material, striped like a bed-ticking, secured to his body with a red belt, from which a hatchet was suspended, was assisting him in " spancelling" a refractory pony. The young gentleman, as I afterward learned, *belonged* to the tribe—some runaway apprentice, perhaps, who thought he was playing Rolla. The rest of the mongrel concern dodged like beavers beneath the mats of their smoky wigwams, as I approached their common fire to warm myself.

Returning to the farm-house, I found a little girl playing on the floor with several strings of beads, which the squaw first mentioned had just parted with to purchase food for her starving infant. The family, however, though they suffered the child to

* See note Q.

retain the ornaments, supplied the poor woman with food and comforts to ten times their value. The Indian mother, I was told, though nearly fainting from exhaustion, asked for nothing except for her child ; and seemed deeply affected when after, by signs, apprizing the whites of her situation, she obtained the required sustenance.

Upon emerging from this grove and getting out once more on the prairie, I could distinguish a solitary horseman, followed by his dog, coming towards us, at least a mile off; and remarking that as they approached us the distance between the man and his canine companion increased at a very unusual rate, I was induced to scan the appearance of the latter as he passed within rifle-shot of our sleigh after his master was out of hail. It proved to be an enormous wolf; and we actually tracked the fellow for eighteen miles, to a thick brake on the banks of a frozen stream, from which he had first leaped into the traveller's tracks, and steadily followed on in his horse's steps to the point where he passed us. The cowardly rascal, being hard pushed with hunger, though he could have no idea of attacking the traveller by himself, had probably just trudged along mile after mile in hope of raising a *posse comitatus* of his long-haired brethren along the road, or of availing himself after nightfall of some accident that might overtake the horseman, who was so unconscious of his volunteer escort. Had the man but turned his horse and run the wolf a hundred yards, he would have rid himself of a companion that circumstances might possibly have rendered inconvenient.

It was late in the afternoon when we reached the banks of Rock River, whose broad and limpid current was, of course, congealed by the rigours of winter. The enterprising and intelligent settler from the city of New-York, who, though repeatedly driven off by the Indians, has been for fifteen years established at " Dixon's Ferry," detained me some time at dinner in expatiating upon the healthfulness of the adjacent country, and the abundance of fish and game of all kinds which frequent the waters of the fine stream upon which he resides. The river, which is navigable for boats of fifty tons nearly a hundred miles above the Mississippi, flows through a gentle valley, with the prairie sloping to its edge upon either side, except when a group of bold rocks, forming a cave, whose entrance has a perfect Gothic arch of some twenty feet high, rear their sudden pinnacles above the farther bank. The smoothness of the adjacent ground is broken here and there by an open grove, while an occasional thicket, with one or two rankly overgrown alluvial islands in the river, must constitute a beautiful landscape in summer. This spot was General Atkinson's head-quarters during the Black Hawk war, and may be considered about the centre of operations during the recent Indian difficulties. A sharp ride of twelve miles over the open prairie brought us after dark to Buffalo Grove, the scene of some of the most melancholy incidents that attended those commotions.

A party of four or five mounted travellers, bound from Galena for the lower country, were obliged to pass the grove on their route just after the difficulties with the Indians commenced. They had reached the edge of the grove, when one of the number, conceiving that it might harbour an ambush, suggested the expediency of deviating from the usual path, and taking a somewhat circuitous course. He was opposed, however, by his companions; and one of them, taunting him with an unnecessary regard to prudence, spurred his horse and advanced first into the fatal wood. His horse could have made but a few bounds—I have seen his grave, just within the edge of the grove—when an Indian bullet brought him to the ground; and his companions, wheeling on their track, for the present escaped further mischief. On arriving at Dixon's Ferry, it was proposed the next day to

return and bury the poor fellow, who had thus
fallen a victim to his own rashness. Eight persons, among whom was Mr. Savary, the Indian
agent for the hostile tribes, volunteered upon the
kind office, which was performed without molesta-
tion, and the agent, with the greater part of those
present, then kept on his way to the upper country; the rest, among whom was my informant,
returning to their home on Rock River. A confused account is given of what followed; as four
of Mr. Savary's party, including himself, were
slain in another ambush; and those who escaped
by the speed of their horses had but little opportunity, after the first surprise, to observe how their
companions met their fate. It is agreed, however,
that the unfortunate agent, turning in his saddle
after the first fire, was shot in the act of appealing
to the Indians as their friend and "father,"—the
reply being a disclaimer of his official character,
and the words, "We have no longer any white
father," accompanying the discharge of the piece
whose bullet pierced his brain. The head of the
ill-fated gentleman, carried off by the Indians, is
said to have been afterward recognised and recovered from the savage band. The Indians fired
the house of the settler (an old New-Yorker) at
Buffalo Grove, and the half-burnt timbers and lonely

door-posts contrasted strangely, as I viewed them in passing, by the morning sun, with the neat new log-dwelling a few paces off, in which I had most comfortably spent the night before.

But these traces of savage war soon, by their frequency, become familiar.

The aspect of the country changes considerably soon after passing Rock River. The prairie is frequently broken by sudden ravines; the number of groves increases; the streams run more rapidly over their pebbly beds; and huge masses of crumbling rock rise like the ruined walls of old castles along the mimic vales through which they take their way. In these secluded dells a number of settlers had ventured to fix themselves along the Galena route; and though many have now returned to their precarious homes, the humble dwellings and various little improvements of others remain as they left them when fleeing with their families before the dreaded savage. With the appearance of one of these cottages I was struck particularly. The roots of a large tree, whose branches brushed a wall of rock opposite to it, had caused a sparkling brook to describe the form of a horse-shoe in winding through a small alluvial bottom, while a row of wild plum-trees across the little peninsula thus formed divided it from the rest of the valley, and just left room enough for the cabin of the settler, with a few acres for a garden around his door. A few acres more along the margin of the brook supplies another enclosure; and the fences and fixtures exhibited a degree of care and arrangement by no means common in this region. But the exiled owner had never returned to his tasteful though humble home. The open door swung loose upon a single hinge. The snow lay far within the threshold; and a solitary raven, perched upon the roof, seemed to consider the abode of desolation so much his own, that, heedless of a flock of his brothers which rose from some carrion near, as we approached the place, he only moved sideways along the rafter, and gave a solitary croak as we drove by.

Approaching Galena, the country becomes still more broken and rocky, until at last a few short hills, here called "knobs," indicated our approach to Fever River; the river itself at once became visible when we had wound round the last of these, and got among the broken ravines that seam the declivity, sloping down for nearly a mile to its margin. Short sudden hills, the bluffs of the prairie beyond, partly wooded and partly faced with rock, formed the opposite shore, while the town of

Galena lay scattered along their broken outline, as
if some giant had pitched a handful of houses
against the hill-side, and the slimy mud (for which
the streets of Galena are celebrated) had caused
them to stick there.   We crossed on the ice, and
I am now once more in a frame-house.

LETTER XXII.

Prairie du Chien, Upper Mississippi, Feb. 5th.

I had only been in Galena a few hours, when I learned that a mail-carrier was to start in the morning for Fort Crawford on the Upper Mississippi, and determined at once to accompany him; deferring an examination of the country around Galena till my return.   It was about eleven o'clock of a fine clear cold day, when my *compagnon de voyage*, a bluff-faced curly-pated fellow, in a green blanket coat, drove up to the door in a better sleigh than I had seen on any of the post-routes below; and wrapping myself up in a couple of buffalo robes and sundry blankets, I found myself, after ascending the rugged bluffs of Fever River, armed at all points to encounter the biting wind which swept the open plain beyond.   And here I may remark, that although the cold winds in this prairie country have a power that I had no idea of till I experienced it, yet the people dress so much more rationally than they do at the North on the sea-board, that health and even comfort are but little invaded. I remember, when first overtaken by the cold weather on the prairies, I was travelling with a simple furred wrapper as an overcoat and a pair of carpet socks over my boots; the last of which, from their clumsy and effeminate appearance, I long neglected to put on. But on arriving one night at a lonely shanty, I found an old Indian trader just disencumbering himself of his travelling gear, and the lesson has not been readily forgotten. His disrobing reminded me of the grave-digger in Hamlet with his sixteen jackets (a stale joke, by-the-by, which is now rarely practised upon the stage),—and a man-at-arms of the fifteenth century, with his armour of plate and triple coat of twisted mail, was not cased in better proof than was my Indian trader. Among the articles of dress that I recollect were a blanket-coat over an ordinary surtout, a plaid cloak upon that, and a buffalo robe trumping the whole; while three pair of woollen socks, buckskin moccasins, and long boots of buffalo-skin with the fur inside, assisted his leggins of green baize in keeping his extremities warm; and a huge hood and visor of fur set Jack Frost at defiance should he assail from above. I do not by any means mention all these defences as constituting the ordinary apparel of the country; for every one on the frontiers dresses just as he pleases, and whether he has his blankets and skins made up into coats and boots, or wears them loose about his person, no one comments upon it. The utmost freedom of dress prevails; and you may see the same person three days in succession with a leather hunting-shirt, a surtout of scarlet woollen, or a coat of superfine broadcloth just from St. Louis, all worn in any company with the same air of independence; and while several colours and textures frequently combine in the same dress, the result is of course an outrageous violation of taste in individual instances, but great picturesqueness of costume upon the whole: the very figure whose apparel is most obnoxious to the laws of good taste as last enacted by fashion, being often that which, of all others, a painter would introduce into a landscape to relieve its colours, or copy for some romantic charm of its own.

The country through which we now drove, though only interspersed here and there with woodland, presented a very different appearance from the open prairie below. In the vicinity of Galena it was much broken by rocky ravines and deep gullies—which, in the spring of the year, must afford a ready passage for the water created by the melting of large bodies of snow; and far away towards the Mississippi, the inequalities of the surface showed like a distant range of mountains, that on nearer approach resolved themselves into three or four distinct hills, which again on reaching their banks proved to be only rocky eminences, of a few hundred feet elevation—standing isolated on the vast plain, like excrescences thrown up by some eruption from its surface. Beyond these, again, the country became beautifully undulating ; and when the warm light of sunset glanced along the tall yellow grass which raised its tapering spears above the snowy surface, and the purple light of evening deepened in the scattered groves that rested on its bosom, it required no exercise of fancy to conceive that these were sloping lawns, and smooth meadows, and open parks, which the gathering shades of night were stealing from the eye. But at last, just where the landscape was becoming almost too broken to keep up these associations of high cultivation, a distant light appeared glimmering at the bottom of a rocky valley, and slipping and floundering through the snow which partially smoothed the rugged descent, we entered a small hamlet of log-huts, and drove up to the door of a frame-building, which proved to be the public-house of " Mineral Point."

A portly Tennesseean, of some six feet high, received us warmly at the door, and hurried me into

a room where a large fire of bur-oak, and a smoking supper of venison and hot corn-cakes were
alike welcomed.   Half a dozen miners in leather
shirts or belted coats of Kentucky jean were
lounging about the establishment, while a tall back-
woodsman in a fringed hunting-frock was stretched
on several chairs, with a pipe in one hand, and the
other resting on a Pelham novel, which, with a
volume of Shakspeare, an old Bible, and the
" Western Songster," formed a pyramid beneath
his brawny arm.   " Whirling Thunder," the Winnebago chief, had, as I was informed, just left the
establishment, or our party would have been perfect.   The old fellow, who, I presume, is superan-
nuated, had been breathing revenge and slaughter
against the Sauks and Foxes, who, he says, have
killed a number of his tribe, and he avows a determination to come down upon the enemy with seven
hundred warriors, though I believe it is well known
that there are not at present half the number in his
tribe, and they scattered far and wide on their hunting expeditions.*   As it was, however, I found the

* The animosity existing between these warlike tribes, it would
seem, has lately manifested itself beneath the very guns of Fort
Crawford.   In an article which appeared in the St. Louis papers
while these pages were passing through the press, it is stated,
under date of November 18th, that " The Indians in the vicinity

company into which I was thrown in more than one way agreeable. They were civil and conversable ; and when a cigar was handed me by a well-

---

of Prairie du Chien have again been engaged in hostile acts, which portend a serious termination. A party of Sauks and Foxes, after killing several Menominies on Grant River, attacked a lodge of Winnebagoes on an island about three miles above Prairie du Chien. It was occupied at the time by women and children only, the warriors being absent on a hunting excursion. Suddenly the Sauk and Fox party made their appearance before the lodge, fired into it, tomahawked and scalped *ten* of the inmates. But one of the Sauk warriors lost his life, and that was by the hand of a Winnebago boy, about fifteen years of age. The youth was standing at the door of the lodge, between a younger brother and sister, when two of the warriors made their appearance and fired upon them. Recollecting instantly that an old gun remained in the lodge loaded, he procured it, and awaited the return of the foe, who had retreated for the purpose of reloading their guns. As soon as they appeared before him, he took deliberate aim at one of them, fired, and the bullet went through the heart of his enemy. He then escaped at the interior of the lodge, made his way for the river, swam it, and gave information of the massacre at Fort Crawford. A detachment of troops was immediately ordered out in pursuit of the murderers, but, as far as known, without success. The Winnebagoes, it is said, had determined on retaliation, and their warriors were already collecting. Their foe, it is also known, are ready to receive them,— having been recently arming and equipping themselves for fight. Towards the Winnebagoes all parties of the Sauks and Foxes have an undying hatred. They view them as having been the cause, by their bad counsels, of all the calamities brought upon dressed gentleman engaged in the mines, who had sat down to supper with us, I stretched my legs before the fire, and soon felt myself perfectly at home. The rumours of Indian wars, with the incidents in those already gone by, being thoroughly discussed, feats of strength and activity were next introduced ; whereat, a burly broad-shouldered fellow, with a head of hair like a boat's swab, jumped on his feet, and shaking the flaps of his rough kersey doublet like a pair of wings, he crowed and swore that he could throw any man of his weight in the mines. " Why, Bill Armstrong," cried a little old man, who I was assured was nearly eighty years of age, shaking the ashes from his pipe the while, " I could double up two such fellows as you in my time ; and I think as it is (slowly rising and collaring the puissant Bill), I'll whip one of them now, for a treat ;" they grappled at once, and Armstrong good-naturedly allowing the old man to put him down, a laugh was raised at his expense. But Bill was too much a cock of the walk to mind it, and striding up to the bar, he called out, " Come here, old fellow, and take your

them by the late war, and as having acted a treacherous and infamous part at the termination of it. Many circumstances concur to make it more than probable, that, should a conflict take place, it will be a long and bloody one."

treat—you're a steamboat; but who couldn't be beat by a fellow that had forty years the advantage of him."

The next day's sun found us, when a few hours high, in a country which, though not a house was to be seen for miles, I can only compare, with its intermingling of prairies and groves, rocky ravines and rapid brooks of sparkling water, to the appearance which the beautiful cultivated districts along the Hudson would present, if the fences and farmhouses were taken away. Its varied aspect was far more pleasing to my eye than the immense plains of table-land below, where the sound of a water-fall is never to be heard, and a stone larger than a pebble is (unless on the banks of the Illinois) rarely met with. The soil, indeed, is not so rich, but the country is unquestionably more healthy; and though the climate is actually more severe in winter, yet the wind is so much broken by the numerous groves, and the general inequalities of surface, that one suffers much less from cold. A great error is committed by government in keeping the wild land of this region out of market, for the patches of woodland, though frequent, are not so dense as those below; and the number of smelting furnaces of lead ore, which are scattered over the whole country, between Rock River and the

Ouisconsin tends to diminish them so rapidly, that a dozen years hence sufficient wood will hardly be left for the ordinary purposes of the farmer. Whatever measures are adopted, however—and I believe there is a bill in relation to these lands now pending in Congress—the pre-emption rights of the first settlers should be secured in the most liberal manner. Their sufferings from three Indian wars within ten years, and their endurance of every risk and privation, are almost incredible ; and, considering that it will take them some time now to recover from the last affair of Black Hawk, government ought to give them several years' credit ; but the early sale of the lands I believe to be indispensable to the future welfare of one of the finest regions in the world. The truth is, that no smelting should be done in the interior, but the mineral should be transported to points where fuel is more abundant, and the timber now growing upon the spot left for the use of the farmers and the miners, to whom it is indispensable for the prosecution of their labours. Such will hardly be the case until a property in lands is established, and individuals are no longer permitted to sweep grove after grove from the soil, till the country begins to assimilate in some places to those leafless

tracts in Illinois, which will probably remain unsettled prairie for a century to come.

I was particularly struck with the bold life
which these miners have long led—the chief dan-
gers of which, it is presumed, are now over—by
observing a strong block-house erected among a
cluster of small shantees where two brothers lived,
with whom we stopped to take some refreshment
at noon. They were miners and farmers together;
and carrying on their business remote from any
other house or settlement, they probably sent the
mineral and vegetable productions of their favoured
soil to market at Galena in the same car. They
had struck the vein of ore which they were working in badger-hunting—the habits of that animal
being of great assistance to the miner in exploring
for mineral. I saw at the same place a fine dog
terribly gored by a wild boar—the descendant of
the domestic hog, which runs wild in this region,
and sometimes makes a good hunt.

Our route hither, which was by no means direct,
carried us through a broken savage country, where
a thousand clear streams seemed to have their birth
among the rocks—singing away—though the earth
was wrapped

" In sap-consuming winter's drizzled snow,"

as if the leaves of June quivered over their crystal currents. At one time these crisped fountains were the only objects that gave life to a burnt forest through which we rode, where the tall branchless and charred trees stood motionless on the steep hill-side, or lay in wild disorder, as they had tumbled from the rocky heights into a ravine below. Emerging from this desolate region, where the tracks of bears and other wild animals were to be seen on every side, we launched out on one of the loveliest prairies I ever beheld. It was about a mile wide, and not more than four or five in length, and smooth as a billiard-table, with two small islets of wood in the centre. Our horses, which had seemed almost fagged out while slipping and stumbling among the rocks and fallen trees in the timbered land, now pricked up their ears and snorted with animation, as they made our light sleigh skim over the smooth plain.

It was afternoon on the third day after leaving Galena, that on descending an abrupt *steppe* of about fifty yards, we came to a small tributary of the Ouisconsin, winding through a narrow valley below. Following down the slender rill, whose banks exhibited no shrubbery save a few dwarf willows, we crossed a wooded bottom, where the long grass among the trees shot above the snow to the height of our horses' shoulders, and reached at last the Ouisconsin, where the stream might be near a quarter of a mile wide. After trying the ice in several places with long poles, we ventured at last to cross; and scaling a bold bluff at the opposite side, paused a moment at a trading-house, owned by a Frenchman, to let our horses blow. A band of Winnebagoes were standing at the door; and as they were all in mourning for some recently-deceased relations,* their broad blunt features, blackened as they were, made them look like Hottentots. A ride of six miles, through a high rolling prairie, interspersed with open groves of oak, brought us at last in view of the bluffs of the upper Mississippi, rising in rocky masses to the height of four or five hundred feet above the bed of that beautiful river, whose iron-bound banks and gentle crystalline current bear but little affinity to the marshy shores and turbid tide which are distinguished by the same name, after the Missouri gives a new character to its waters. Never shall I forget the first view of " The Father of Rivers," as a reach of several miles—shut in, partly by its own bluffs, and partly by those of the Ouisconsin, with its numerous islets smiling in the light of the setting sun —stretched like some comely lake of the west

* See note R.

before my eye. It was girdled, apparently, by
inaccessible cliffs on three sides, and fringed by
a broad meadow—which in its turn was bounded
and sheltered by lofty bluffs—on the fourth.   That
meadow lay now beneath me,—and it was Prairie
du Chien.

APPENDIX.

Note A.—*Page* 56.

THE story of Adam Poe's desperate encounter with two Indians, as told in "Metcalf's Indian Warfare of the West," is one of the most characteristic traditions of the Ohio.

It was about the close of the Revolution that a party of six or seven Wyandot Indians crossed over to the south side of the Ohio River, fifty miles below Pittsburg, and in their hostile excursions among the early settlers killed an old man, whom they found alone in one of the houses which they plundered. The news soon spread among the white people; seven or eight of whom seized their rifles, and pursued the marauders. In this party were two brothers, named Adam and Andrew Poe, strong and active men, and much respected in the settlement. They followed up the chase all night, and in the morning found themselves, as they expected, upon the right track. The Indians could now be easily followed by their traces on the dew. The print of one very large foot was seen, and it was thus known that a famous Indian of uncommon size and strength must be of the party. The track led to the river. The whites followed it directly, Adam Poe excepted; who, fearing that they might be taken by surprise, broke off from the rest. His intention was to creep along the edge of the bank under cover of the trees and bushes, and to fall upon the savages so suddenly that he might get them between his own fire and that of his companions. At the point where he suspected they were, he saw the rafts which they were accustomed to push before them when they swam the river, and on which they placed their blankets, tomahawks, and guns. The Indians themselves he could not see, and was obliged to go partly down the bank to get a shot at them. As he descended with his rifle cocked, he discovered two—the celebrated large Indian and a smaller one, separated from the others, and holding their rifles also cocked in their hands. He took aim at the large one, but his rifle snapped, without giving the intended fire. The Indians turned instantly at the sound. Poe was too near them to retreat, and had not time to cock and take aim again. Suddenly he leaped down upon them, and caught the large Indian by the clothes, on his breast, and the small one by throwing an arm round his neck: they all fell together, but Poe was uppermost. While he was struggling to keep down the large Indian, the small one, at a word spoken by his fellow-savage, slipped his neck out of Poe's embrace, and ran to the raft for a tomahawk. The large Indian at this moment threw his arms about Poe's body, and held him fast, that the other might come up and kill him. Poe watched the approach and the descending arm of the small Indian so well, that at the instant of the intended stroke he raised his foot, and by a vigorous and skilful blow knocked the tomahawk from the assailant's hand. At this, the large Indian cried out with an exclamation of contempt for the small one. The latter, however, caught his tomahawk again and approached more cautiously, waving his arm up and down with mock blows, to deceive Poe as to the stroke which was intended to be real and fatal. Poe, however, was so vigilant and active that he averted the tomahawk from his head, and received it upon his wrist with a considerable wound, deep enough to cripple but not entirely to destroy the use of his hand. In this crisis of peril he made a violent effort, and broke loose from the large Indian. He snatched a rifle, and shot the small one as he ran up a third time with his lifted tomahawk. The large Indian was now on his feet, and grasping Poe by the shoulder and the leg, hurled him in the air, heels over head upon the shore. Poe instantly rose, and a new and more desperate struggle ensued. The bank was slippery, and they fell into the water, when each strove to drown the other. Their efforts were long and doubtful, each alternately under and half-strangled; until Poe, fortunately, grasped with his unwounded hand the tuft of hair upon the scalp of the Indian, and forced his head into the water. This appeared to be decisive of his fate, for soon he manifested all the symptoms of a drowning man, bewildered in the moment of death. Poe relaxed his hold, and discovered too late the stratagem. The Indian was instantly upon his feet again, and engaged anew in the fierce contest for victory and life. They were naturally carried farther into the stream, and the current becoming stronger bore them beyond their depth. They were now compelled to loosen their hold upon each other, and to swim for mutual safety. Both sought the shore to seize a gun ; but the Indian was the best swimmer, and gained it first. Poe then turned immediately back into the water to avoid a greater danger—meaning to dive, if possible, to escape the fire. Fortunately for him, the Indian caught up the rifle which had been discharged into the breast of the smaller savage. At this critical juncture Poe's brother Andrew presented himself. He had just left the party who had been in pursuit of the other Indians, and who had killed all but one of them at the expense of three of their own lives. He had heard that Adam was in great peril, and alone in a fight with two against him ; for one of the whites had mistaken Adam in the water with his bloody hand for a wounded Indian, and fired a bullet into his shoulder. Adam now cried out to his brother to kill the big Indian on the shore ; but Andrew's gun had been discharged, and was not again loaded. The contest was now between the savage and Andrew. Each laboured to load his rifle first. The Indian, after putting in his powder, and hurrying his motions to force down the ball, drew out his ramrod with such violence as to throw it some yards into the water. While he ran to pick it up, Andrew gained an advantage, as the Indian had still to ram his bullet home. But a hair would have turned the scale ; for the savage was just raising his gun to his eye with unerring aim, when he received the fatal fire of the backwoodsman. Andrew then jumped into the river to assist his wounded brother to the shore ; but Adam, thinking more of carrying the big Indian home, as a trophy, than of his own wounds, urged Andrew to go back and prevent the struggling savage from rolling himself into the current and escaping. Andrew, however, was too solicitous for the fate of Adam to allow him to obey ; and the high-souled Wyandot, jealous of his honour as a warrior, even in death, and knowing well the intention of his white conquerors, succeeded in retaining life and action long enough to reach the current, by which his dead body was swept down beyond the chance of pursuit.

[The above account is abridged from the narrative given in the interesting compilation published in early life by Dr. Samuel L. Metcalf—since better known as the ingenious author of " A New Theory of Magnetism," " Molecular Attractions," &c. The work is believed to be out of print ; and it is a subject of regret that Dr. M., who was born among the scenes celebrated in these wild narratives, cannot find time amid his graver researches to give his youthful publication in a new dress to the world.]

NOTE B.—*Page* 63.

Colonel James Smith, of the provincial forces, who was a prisoner in Fort Du Quesne at the time, and saw the attacking party march out to Braddock's Field, estimates their number at even less. The following is his account (as published in 1799) of what passed in the Fort immediately previous and subsequent to the conflict.

" On the 9th day of July, 1755, I heard a great stir in the Fort. As I could then walk with a staff in my hand, I went out of the door which was just by the wall of the Fort, and stood upon the wall, and viewed the Indians in a huddle before the gate, where were barrels of powder, bullets, flints, &c., and every one taking what suited ; I saw the Indians also march off in rank entire ; likewise the French, Canadians, and some regulars. After viewing the Indians and French in different positions, I computed them to be about four hundred, and wondered that they attempted to go out against Braddock with so small a party. I was then in high hopes that I would soon see them flying before the British troops, and that General Braddock would take the Fort and rescue me. I remained anxious to know the event of this day ; and in the afternoon I again observed a great noise and commotion in the Fort ; and though at that time I could not understand much, yet I found that it was the voice of joy and triumph, and found that they had received what I called bad news. I had observed some of the old country soldiers speak Dutch ; and as I spoke

Dutch, I went to one of them and asked him what was the news. He told me that a runner had just arrived, who said that Braddock would certainly be defeated ; that the Indians and French had surrounded him, and were concealed behind trees and in gullies, and kept a constant fire upon the English, and that they saw the English falling in heaps ; and if they did not take the river, which was the only gap, and make their escape, there would not be one man left alive before sunset. Some time after this I heard a company of Indians and French coming in : I observed that they had a great many bloody scalps, grenadiers' caps, British canteens, bayonets, &c., with them. They brought the news that Braddock was defeated. After that, another company came in, which appeared to be about one hundred, and chiefly Indians ; and it seemed to me that almost every one of this company was carrying scalps : after this came another company, with a number of wagon-horses and also a great many scalps. Those that were coming in and those that had arrived kept a constant firing of small-arms, and also the great guns in the Fort, which were accompanied with the most hideous shouts and yells from all quarters, so that it appeared to me as if the infernal regions had broken loose. About sunset I beheld a small party coming in with about a dozen prisoners, stripped naked, with their hands tied behind their backs, and their faces and part of their bodies blacked. These prisoners they burnt to death on the banks of the Alleghany River, opposite to the Fort. I stood on the Fort wall until I beheld them begin to burn one of these men. They had tied him to a stake, and kept touching him with firebrands, red-hot irons, &c., and he screaming in a most doleful manner ; the Indians in the mean time yelling like infernal spirits. As this scene appeared too shocking for me to behold, I returned to my lodging both sore and sorry."—*A Narrative of the most remarkable Occurrences in the Life and Travels of Colonel James Smith, during his Captivity among the Indians, from the year* 1755 *until* 1759.

Note C.—*Page* 133.

It was in this battle that the noble Tecumseh fell—dying, as it was supposed, by a pistol-shot from Col. Johnson. If Thatcher's

Indian Biography has not already made the reader familiar with
the career of this famous savage, he is referred to Mr. Schoolcraft's Travels, where an authentic account of Tecumseh, interspersed with many characteristic anecdotes, will be found. There
s also a succinct biographical sketch of him in the Encyclopædia
Americana, which concludes by summing up his qualities as
follows :—

" Tecumseh was a remarkable man, fitted for obtaining greatness both in peace and war. His eloquence was vivid and powerful. He was sagacious in contriving and accomplishing his objects, and by his address obtained an unlimited influence over his
savage brethren. Throughout life he was exemplary in his habits
of temperance and adherence to truth. He was disinterested,
generous, hospitable, and humane. He married at a mature age
in consequence of the persuasions of his friends, and left one
child. In person he was about five feet ten inches high, with
handsome features, a symmetrical and powerful frame, and an air
of dignity and defiance."

Note D.—*Page* 164.

" The Ottawas say that there are two great Beings that rule
and govern the universe, who are at war with each other,—the
one they call *Maneto* and the other *Matche-Maneto.* They say
that Maneto is all kindness and love, and that Matche-Maneto is
an evil spirit that delights in doing mischief ; and some of them
think that they are equal in power, and therefore worship the
evil spirit out of a principle of fear. Others doubt which of
the two may be the most powerful, and therefore endeavour to
keep in favour with both, by giving each of them some kind of
worship. Others say that Maneto is the first great cause, and
therefore must be all-powerful and supreme, and ought to be
adored and worshipped ; whereas Matche-Maneto ought to be
rejected and despised."—*Col. Smith's Narrative.*

Note E.—*Page* 201.

" The Pottawattamies, whose name, as sounded by themselves,
is Po-ta-wà-tó-mi (in their language, ' We are making Fire'),

appear to be connected, not only by language, but also by their manners, customs, and opinions, with the numerous nations of Algonquin origin. * * * * * * * * *
Their notions of religion appear to be of the most simple kind—they believe in the existence of an only God, whom they term Kasha-Maneto, or Great Spirit. Kasha means great, and Maneto an irresistible being. The epithet of Kasha is never applied to any other word but as connected with the Supreme Being."

[Here, with a more minute account of the usages of this tribe, follows an examination of the charge of *cannibalism*, brought against the Pottawattamies by numerous travellers.]

" The Pottawattamies have a number of war-songs, formed for the most part of one or two ideas, expressed in short and forcible sentences, which they repeat over and over in a low humming kind of tune, which to our ears appeared very monotonous : they have no love-songs ; the business of singing (among them*) being *always* connected with warlike avocations. Singing is always attended by the dance. The only musical instruments which they use are the drum, rattle, and a kind of *flageolet*. Their games are numerous and diversified ; they resemble many of those known to civilized men—such as gymnastic exercises, battledore, pitching the bar, ball, tennis, and cup-ball, for which they use the spur of the deer with a string attached to it.

" The Pottawattamies are, for the most part, well-proportioned ; about five feet eight inches in height ; possessed of much muscular strength in the arm, but rather weak in the back, with a strong neck ; endowed with considerable agility."

[The above is from Major Long's Second Expedition, performed by order of the secretary of war, in 1823. The number of the Pottawattamies was then estimated at about three thousand.]

According to the information of one of their chiefs, " the Pottawattamies believe that they came from the vicinity of the Sault de St. Marie, where they presume that they were created. A singular belief which they entertain is, that the souls of the departed have, on their way to the great prairie, to cross a large stream, over which a log is placed as a bridge, but that this is in such constant agitation that none but the spirits of good men can pass

* It is otherwise at least with the Ottawas, Chippewas, and Menomonés.

over it in safety ; while those of the bad slip from the log into the water, and are never after heard of. This information they pretend to have had revealed to them by one of their ancestors, who, being dead, travelled to the edge of the stream, but not liking to venture on the log, determined to return to the land of the living ; which purpose he effected, having been seen once more among his friends two days after his reputed death. He informed them of what he had observed, and further told them that, while on the verge of the stream, he had heard the sounds of the drum, to the beat of which the blessed were dancing on the opposite prairie."
—*Narrative of an Expedition to the Source of St. Peter's River, by W. H. Keating, A.M.,* &c.

Note F.—*Page* 202.

" In descending the Ontonagon River, which falls into Lake Superior, our Indian guides stopped on the east side of the river to examine a bear-fall that had been previously set, and were overjoyed to find a large bear entrapped. As it was no great distance from the river, we all landed to enjoy the sight. The animal sat upon his fore-paws, facing us, the hinder paws being pressed to the ground by a heavy weight of logs, which had been arranged in such a manner as to allow the bear to creep under ; and when, by seizing the bait, he had sprung the trap, he could not extricate himself, although with his fore-paws he had demolished a part of the work. After viewing him for some time, a ball was fired through his head, but did not kill him. The bear kept his position, and seemed to growl in defiance. A second ball was aimed at the heart, and took effect ; but he did not resign the contest immediately, and was at last despatched with an axe. As soon as the bear fell, one of the Indians walked up, and addressing him by the name of Muckwah, shook him by the paw with a smiling countenance, saying, in the Indian language, he was sorry he had been under the necessity of killing him, and hoped that the offence would be forgiven, particularly as Long Knife (an American) had fired one of the balls."—*Schoolcraft's Journal.*

Note G.—*Page* 203.

" The Ottawas have a very useful kind of tents which they

carry with them, made of flags platted and stitched together in a very artful manner, so as to turn rain or wind well. Each mat is made fifteen feet long, and about five broad. In order to erect this kind of tent, they cut a number of long straight poles, which they drive in the ground in the form of a circle, leaning inwards; then they spread the mats on these poles, beginning at the bottom and extending up, leaving only a hole in the top uncovered, and this hole answers the place of a chimney. They make a fire of dry split wood in the middle, and spread down bark-mats and skins for bedding, on which they sleep in a crooked posture all round the fire, as the length of their beds will not admit of their stretching themselves. In place of a door, they lift up one end of a mat, and creep in and let the mat fall down behind them. These tents are warm and dry, and tolerably clear of smoke. Their lumber they keep under birch-bark canoes, which they carry out and turn up for a shelter, when they keep every thing from the rain. Nothing is in the tents but themselves and their bedding."—*Col. Smith's Narrative.*

Note H.—*Page* 225.

" The Carey Mission-house, so designated in honour of the late Mr. Carey, the indefatigable apostle of India, is situated within about a mile of the river, and twenty-five miles (by land) above its mouth. The ground upon which it is erected is the site of an ancient and extensive Potawatomi village, now no longer in existence. The establishment was instituted by the Baptist Missionary Society in Washington, and is under the superintendence of the Rev. Mr. M'Coy, a man whom, from all the reports we heard of him, we should consider as very eminently qualified for the important trust committed to him. The plan adopted in the school proposes to unite a practical with an intellectual education. The boys are instructed in the English language, in reading, writing, and arithmetic. They are made to attend to the usual occupations of a farm, and to perform every occupation connected with it—such as ploughing, planting, harrowing, &c. : in these pursuits they appear to take great delight. The system being well regulated, they find time for every thing, not only for study and labour, but also for innocent recreation, in which they are encouraged to indulge. The females receive in the school the same instruction which is given to the boys, and are, in addition to this, taught spinning, weaving, and sewing (both plain and ornamental. They were just beginning to embroider—an occupation which may by some be considered as unsuitable to the situation which they are destined to hold in life ; but which appears to us to be very judiciously used as a reward and stimulus : it encourages their taste and natural talent for imitation, which is very great ; and by teaching them that occupation may be connected with amusement, prevent their relapsing into indolence. They are likewise made to attend to the pursuits of the dairy, such as the milking of cows, churning of milk, &c. The establishment is intended to be opened for children from seven to fourteen years old ; they very properly receive them at a much earlier age, and even—where a great desire of learning was manifested —older persons have been admitted. All appear to be very happy, and to make as rapid progress as white children of the same age would make. Their principal excellence rests in works of imitation ; they write astonishingly well, and many display great natural talent for drawing. The institution receives the countenance of the most respectable among the Indians, who visit the establishment occasionally, appear pleased with it, and show their favour to it by presents of sugar, venison, &c., which they often make to the family of the missionary. The establishment, being sanctioned by the war department, receives annually one thousand dollars from the United States, for the support of a teacher and blacksmith, according to the conditions of the treaty concluded at Chicago in 1821 by Governor Cass and Mr. Sibley, commissioners on the part of the United States."

[The above interesting account of the Carey Mission is abridged from that given in the narrative of Long's expedition. The time that has elapsed since it originally appeared has of course diminished its present value ; but the author not having had an opportunity of visiting the establishment, and finding, from all the inquiries he could make regarding it, that the institution is sustaining itself efficiently upon the plan above detailed, he has thought that it would be more satisfactory to the reader to have this compendium of an official report in the appendix, than to dwell upon any hearsay information which he might have supplied in the text.]

Note I.—*Page* 225.

" They made their winter cabins in the following form: they cut logs about fifteen feet long, and laid these logs upon each other, and drove posts in the ground, at each end, to keep them together; the posts they tied together at the top with bark; and by this means raised a wall fifteen feet long and about four feet high, and in the same manner they raised another wall opposite to this at about twelve feet distance; then they drove forks in the ground in the centre of each end, and laid a strong pole from end to end on these forks; and from these walls to the pole they set up poles instead of rafters, and on these they tied small poles in place of laths, and a cover was made of lynn-bark, which will run (peal) even in the winter-season. At the end of these walls they set up split timber, so that they had timber all round, excepting a door at each end: at the top, in place of a chimney, they left an open place, and for bedding they laid down the aforesaid kind of bark, on which they spread bear-skins: from end to end of this hut, along the middle, there were fires, which the squaws made of dry split wood; and the holes or open places that appeared the squaws stopped with moss, which they collected from old logs, and at the door they hung a bear-skin; and notwithstanding the winters are hard here, our lodging was much better than I expected."—*Col. Smith's Narrative.*

Note J.—*Page* 227.

" In this month we began to make sugar. As some of the elm-bark will strip at this season, the squaws, after finding a tree that would do, cut it down; and with a crooked stick, broad and sharp at the end, took the bark off the tree; and of this bark made vessels in a curious manner, that would hold about two gallons each: they made about one hundred of these kind of vessels. In the sugar-tree they cut a notch, and stuck in a tomahawk: in the place where they stuck the tomahawk they drove a long chip, in order to carry the water out from the tree, and under this they set their vessel to receive it; they also made bark-vessels for carrying

the water, that would hold about four gallons each ; they had **two**
brass-kettles that held about fifteen gallons each, and other smaller
kettles, in which they boiled the water as fast as it was collected ;
they made vessels of bark, that would hold about 100 gallons each,
for containing the water ; and though the sugar-trees did not run
every day, they had always a sufficient quantity of water to keep
them boiling during the whole sugar-season."—*Col. Smith's
Narrative.*

NOTE K.—*Page* 237.

The town of Chicago has become so important a place, and is
so rapidly developing its resources, as to call for a more particular notice than it receives in the text. Its sudden strides to prosperity can be best estimated, however, by first perceiving the condition and prospects of Chicago as they presented themselves to
Major Long's party when they visited it ten years since. " The
village presents no cheering prospect, as, notwithstanding its antiquity, it consists of but few huts, inhabited by a miserable race of
men, scarcely equal to the Indians, from whom they are descended.
Their log or bark-houses are low, filthy, and disgusting, displaying not the least trace of comfort. Chicago is, perhaps, one of
the oldest settlements in the Indian country. A fort is said to
have formerly existed there : mention is made of the place as
having been visited in 1671 by Perot, who found ' Chicagou' to be
the residence of a powerful chief of the Miamis. The number of
trails centring all at this spot, and their apparent antiquity, indicate that this was probably for a long while the site of a large Indian village. As a place of business, it offers no inducement to
the settler ; for the whole annual amount of the trade on the lake
did not exceed the cargo of five or six schooners, even at the time
when the garrison received its supplies from Macikinaw."—
Long's Second Expedition, vol. i. p. 164.

Contrast this desolate picture—not with the representation
made in the text, but—with the existing condition of the place,
with the alterations that have taken place since the writer left
there, not yet a year ago. He is informed by a gentleman recently from Illinois, that Chicago, which but eighteen months
since contained but two or three frame-buildings, and a few miser-

able huts, has now five hundred houses, four hundred of which
have been erected this year, and two thousand two hundred inhabitants. A year ago there was not a place of public worship
in the town; there are now five churches and two school-houses,
and numerous brick stores and warehouses. The shipping-lists
of daily arrivals and departures show how soon the enterprise and
activity of our citizens have discovered and improved the capa-
bilities of that port. There have been three hundred arrivals this
year, and more than $50,000 worth of salt has been sold there
this season, and of European and domestic merchandise to the
amount of $400,000. A line of four steamboats of the largest
class of lake-boats, and regular lines of brigs and schooners, are
now established between that port and the principal ports of the
lower lakes.

It is gratifying to hear of such improvement in the western
country, and to have predictions so recently made of the growth
and prosperity of this point in particular, thus far more than
fulfilled.

Note L.—*Page* 243.

The Indians that frequent the neighbourhood of Chicago (pronounced *Tshicawgo*), though not so numerous, are composed of the
same mixture of different tribes which Major Long noticed ten
years since. They are chiefly Pottawattamies and Ottawas, with
a few Chippewas (ò-chè-pe-wàg) and a straggling Kickapoo or
Miami; and a great admixture of the different languages (or
rather dialects, for they are radically the same) of the three first
prevails there. Among them are many who have borne arms
against the Americans; and some who, doubtless, took a part in
the massacre at the fall of the place in 1812. The particulars of
that bloody affair are yet mentioned with horror by the old settlers.
They may be briefly summed up as follows:—

It was soon after the infamous surrender of General Hull at
Detroit, when, in pursuance of the terms entered into with the
enemy by that officer, who was commandant-in-chief upon the
north-west frontier, Captain Heald, the commandant at Chicago,
prepared to surrender his post to the British. The Pottawattamies, and other hostile Indians in the vicinity, were on the

watch for the movement ; and on the morning when the garrison evacuated the place, they had so completely succeeded in duping Captain Wells, the credulous and unfortunate Indian agent, that the fatal march of the 15th October, 1812, was precipitated by his advice. The Americans were about seventy in number, with several women and children ; and they were escorted from the shelter of the fort by a band of about thirty Miamies. The road led along the beach of the lake, with those short sand-hills spoken of in a previous letter extending along the route between the lake and the open prairie. Behind these the British Indians lay concealed ; and when the Americans had proceeded about a mile from the fort, the wily enemy sprang from his lair, and poured down a murderous fire upon the beach. Captain Heald immediately brought his men to a charge, and drove the Indians from the nearest sand-hill ; but their numbers were so great that they formed instantly again upon his flank. His party was surrounded ; and while the Miamies in a manner withdrew their protection, and helped to swell the number of his opponents, the little force of Captain Heald was completely cut off from the women and children, who were cowering beneath the baggage on the lake-shore. The Americans fought with desperation ; but such a handful of men was soon cut to pieces ; and scarcely a man survived to witness the atrocities that were practised upon the helpless creatures upon the beach. There were four officers killed upon the spot ; Captain Heald and his wife were both badly wounded ; and twelve children* were butchered on the shore, or shared the fate of their mothers, who ran shrieking over the prairie. The unhappy Indian agent, who was among the slain, is said to have had his breast cut open, and his heart roasted and eaten by the savage foe.

Note M.—*Page 245.*

" The Chicago River, which is about two hundred and fifty feet wide, has sufficient depth of water for lake-vessels to where it forks in the centre of the town. The southern and principal branch takes its rise about six miles from the fort in a swamp,

* Captain Heald's Letter, dated Pittsburg, Oct. 23, 1812.

which communicates also with the Des Plaines, one of the head branches of the Illinois. This swamp, which is designated by the Canadian voyageurs as Le Petit Lac, is navigable at certain seasons of the year: it has been frequently travelled by traders in their pirogues; and a batteau from St. Louis, loaded with provisions for the garrison at Chicago, has through this medium passed from the Mississippi into Lake Michigan. Major Long observes, upon passing through this marsh in a canoe, " we were delighted at beholding for the first time a feature so interesting in itself, but which we had afterward an opportunity of observing frequently on the route ; viz. the division of waters starting from the same source and running in two different directions, so as to become the feeders of streams that discharge themselves into the ocean at immense distances apart. * * * * * When we consider the facts above stated, we are irresistibly led to the conclusion, that an elevation of the lakes a few feet (not exceeding ten or twelve) above their present level, would cause them to discharge their waters, partly at least, into the Gulf of Mexico. That such a discharge has at one time existed, every one conversant with the nature of the country must admit ; and it is equally apparent that an expenditure trifling in comparison to the importance of the object would again render Lake Michigan a tributary of the Mexican Gulf."

Note N.—*Page* 269.

Mr. Schoolcraft says that no female captive is ever saved by the Indians from base motives, or need fear the violation of her honour: " The whole history of their wars may be challenged for a solitary instance of the violation of female chastity. When they resolve to spare life, they also resolve to spare that reputation without which life is not worth possessing. They treat them with kindness and attention, carrying them dry across rivers, and directing, what with them is accounted an act of distinguished attention, that their hair shall be combed every morning. The precise reason for this trait of their character has never been fully explained. Innate principles of virtue can hardly be supposed to be sufficient to produce so universal an effect, though it would be uncharitable to deny that they have their share. It is asserted that the Indians believe that the taking such a dishonourable advantage of their female prisoners would have the effect to destroy their luck in hunting. It would be considered as a trait of weakness and effeminacy in a warrior, unworthy of his fame and reputation for manly achievement. It would excite the ridicule of his companions, and, as they believe, be displeasing to the Great Spirit."—*Travels in the Central Portions of the Mississippi Valley, page* 394.

Note O.—*Page* 279.

" *Starved Rock*."—This remarkable isolated hill, termed by the French voyageurs Le Rocher, or Rockfort as Mr. Schoolcraft calls it, is described by that accurate traveller as an elevated cliff on the left bank of the Illinois, consisting of parallel layers of white sandstone. It is not less than two hundred and fifty feet high, perpendicular on three sides, and washed at its base by the river. On the fourth side it is connected with the adjacent range of bluffs by a narrow peninsular ledge, which can only be ascended by a precipitous winding path. The summit of the rock is level, and contains about three-fourths of an acre. It is covered with a soil of several feet in depth, bearing a growth of young trees. Strong and almost inaccessible by nature, this natural battlement was the scene of a desperate conflict between the fierce and haughty Pottawattamies and one band of the Illinois Indians; the latter fled to this place for refuge from the fury of their enemies. The post could not be carried by assault, and tradition says that the besiegers finally attempted, after many repulses, to reduce it by starvation. This siege, as is remarked by a popular writer, is singularly characteristic on either side of those remarkable traits of savage character, undaunted resolution and insatiable and ever vigilant thirst for vengeance. Its result is well told in " Tales of the Border," the newly published work of Judge Hall. The pangs of hunger, the tortures of thirst, pressed upon the besieged ; but they maintained their post with invincible courage, determined rather to die of exhaustion than to afford their enemies the triumph of killing them in battle or exposing them at the stake. Every stratagem which they attempted was discovered and defeated. The scorching sun that beat upon their towering hold maddened them to taste the cool stream that glided beneath it ; but when they endeavoured to procure water during the night by lowering vessels attached to cords of bark into the river, the vigilant besiegers detected the design, and placed a guard in canoes to prevent its execution. They all perished—one, and one only, excepted. The last surviving warriors defended the entrance so well that the enemy could neither enter nor discover the fatal progress of the work of death ; and when at last, all show of resistance having ceased, and all signs of life disappeared, the victors ventured cautiously to approach, they found but one survivor—a squaw, whom they adopted into their own tribe, and who was yet living when the first white man penetrated this region.*

Note P.—*Page* 292.

" The usual dress of the men (among the northern tribes) at the present day consists of a figured cotton shirt ; a blanket, or a French capote of blue cloth ; a pair of blue, green, or red cloth metasses or leggins ; an azeeaun or breech cloth, and moccasins of dressed deer-skin. The metasses are generally ornamented, and a garter of coloured worsted tied around the knee. The front fold of the azeeaun is also ornamented around the edges. A necklace of wampum, or a silver crescent, or both, are often worn together with silver arm-bands and wrist-bands. The latter are not exclusively confined to chiefs, so far as we have observed, but their use depends rather upon the ability of the individual to purchase them. Ear-rings are common to both sexes. A knife is commonly worn in a scabbard confined under the string or narrow belt which sustains both the azeeaun and the metasses. The head is ornamented with a band of skin dressed with the hair or pelt on, surmounted with feathers. In this respect there seems to be less uniformity than in any other part of their costume. Often the head-piece is wanting. Long hair is prevalent. It is sometimes braided, and ornamented with silver brooches. Paints are still used for the face, both for the purposes of dress and mourning. Each Indian youth, from the time he is acknowledged as a hunter, capable of supporting him-

* Charlevoix, Schoolcraft, Hall.

self, ordinarily carries a pipe, and a skipetagun, or tobacco-pouch. This pouch is commonly the entire skin of an otter, lynx, or other small animal, dressed with the pelt on ; and drawing an aperture upon the throat, this sack, besides the usual quantity of tobacco and smoking-weed (kinnekinic), commonly contains a fire-steel, flint, and bit of spunk, and sometimes a knife. But this appendage is not to be confounded with the sacred Meta-wiiaun, or medicine-sack, which is the consecrated repository, not only of his medicines, but also of his personal manitos and relics."—*Schoolcraft's Travels in the Central Portions of the Mississippi Valley.*

Note Q.—*Page* 297.

Robertson, Charlevoix, and other European writers mention that the American Indians have naturally no beards. Mr. School-craft, in observing that a beard is less common to our aborigines than to the natives of Europe or Asia, ascribes its absence chiefly to the fashion of plucking it out in early life. " It is esteemed necessary to the decency of appearance, among the young and middle-aged, to remove the beard ; and as the razor is unknown to them, they employ the only means at command to eradicate it. Hence it is more common to see beards upon old men, who become careless and neglectful of personal appearance. Of the Indians of the Algonquin stock, the Chippewas are perhaps the most exempted from beards, the Ottawas less so, and the Potta-wattamies still less. Among the two last tribes there is a custom sufficiently frequent, though not universal, of letting the beard grow only upon the under lip, or upon the chin, from which it depends in a compact lock, or a kind of bunch."—*Travels in the Mississippi Valley.*

Note R.—*Page* 316.

The Winnebagoes, as they are the most savage-looking, are among the haughtiest of the tribesmen. They differ in many respects from the neighbouring clans ; and Carver says, that in his time there was a tradition in the country that the nation sprung from " some strolling band from the Mexican countries." In

" Long's Expedition" they are mentioned as being of distinct origin from the Algonquin tribes, and their language is said to present greater difficulties than any of the northern dialects. " It abounds," says that work, " in harsh and guttural sounds, and in the letter *r*, which does not appear to be common in the Algonquin languages. It is difficult to obtain correct information concerning the manners and characters of the Winnebagoes, as a strong prejudice appears to prevail against them. They are considered unfriendly to white men, and this, instead of being viewed in the light of a favourable trait of their character, as indicative of a high spirit which can resent injustice and oppression, and which will not crouch before the aggressor, has been the occasion of much ill-will towards them."—*Long's Expedition, page* 216.

The custom of blacking the face by way of mourning, as mentioned in the text, is by no means peculiar to the Winnebagoes :—

" The Indians are particular in their demonstrations of grief for departed friends ; they consist in darkening their faces with charcoal, fasting, abstaining from the use of vermilion, and other ornaments in dress, &c. ; they also make incisions in their arms, legs, and other parts of the body. These are not made for the purposes of mortification, or to create a pain which shall, by dividing their attention, efface the recollection of their loss ; but entirely from a belief that their grief is internal, and that the only way of dispelling it is to give it a vent through which to escape."
—*Ibid, page* 226.